What Does a Progressive Christian Believe?

A Guide for the Searching, the Open, and the Curious

by
Delwin Brown

SEABURY BOOKS
an imprint of
Church Publishing Incorporated, New York

Cover design by Lindy Gifford
Interior design by Ronda Scullen

Library of Congress Cataloging-in-Publication Data

Brown, Delwin, 1935–
    What does a progressive Christian believe? : a guide for the searching, the open, and the curious / by Delwin Brown.
        p. cm.
    Includes bibliographical references.
    ISBN 978-1-59627-084-8 (pbk.)
    1. Liberalism (Religion) I. Title.

BR1615.B76 2008
230'.046—dc22
                                        2007043198

Church Publishing, Incorporated.
445 Fifth Avenue
New York, New York 10016

www.churchpublishing.com

5 4 3 2 1

Christmas, 2009

I found this to keep me focused and encouraged on the journey — + I wanted to share it with you.

For our grandchildren

Stella Rae
Sophie Elizabeth
Cody Benjamin
Georgia Anne
Emma Nayali

and the far better world they deserve

Merry Christmas !
Love,
Anne

Contents

Acknowledgments

If it takes a village to raise a child, at least that many people are needed to write a book. Here, though, I have space to thank by name only the most immediate contributors to this endeavor. In a parking lot after a lecture in Alabama, Ernest Stokely, president of *South Points Association for Exploring Religion* (*SPAFER*), told me I should write a book like this rather than continuing to write exclusively for academic colleagues. When I recounted this conversation to Steve Swecker, editor of *The Progressive Christian*, he suggested that I post serially a draft of my chapters on a *TPC*-sponsored blog, told me what a "blog" is, and made all of the arrangements necessary for my doing so. A number of readers of the blog made helpful comments. I cannot mention them all, but some deserve explicit credit for their critical responses and/or corrections, especially Walter John Boris, Cythia Astle, Peter Sawtell, Dean Smith, "Chuck," Brook McBride, and Richard Allen. Jennifer Jesse, a young ("progressive Christian," I would say) scholar of great promise, read the manuscript with a sympathetic critic's eye and proposed numerous improvements. Margaret Allen, wonderful colleague with me on the staff of *The Progressive Christian Witness*, was my first reader and editor, for clarity as well as correctness. Janet Carlson, professional editor and friend of years past and to come, gave the manuscript a final pre-submission proofing. Cynthia Shattuck, my editor at Church Publishing, blessed the final stages of this project with editorial efficiency and an insistence on the importance of what I was attempting to do.

The next circle of contributors to this project know who they are: in particular, former colleagues at Pacific School of Religion who supported me as I began to write in this vein for a general audience, and leaders of various grass-roots progressive Christian organizations whose efforts have created the larger context within which I now find myself speaking and writing. They all deserve special thanks for their labors, but here I mention only those whose work I know best, the leaders of *SPAFER*, The Beatitudes Society, Micahs Call, Progressive Christians Uniting, The Center for Progressive Christianity, and, of course, *The Progressive Christian* ("a bi-monthly magazine for people of faith seeking the common good").

Preface

P rogressive Christianity is a family of perspectives that vigorously rejects the "religious right" as a gross distortion of the Christian faith. Just as important, progressive Christianity criticizes and moves beyond the (other) conservatisms and the liberalisms of the immediate Christian past. In our time, it is new. This book presents one progressive Christian standpoint—introductory in character for ordinary people, not specialists.

The conviction that eventually gave rise to this book was born about two o'clock in the morning, the day after the 2004 presidential election. It grew out of the stunned realization that the long tradition of progressive Christian thought and action had virtually disappeared from the public discussion leading up to that election. The progressive Christian voice had not been silenced by others. It had stopped speaking. Or, more accurately, we who are progressive Christians had stopped speaking.

Why had we become silent? There are no doubt several reasons, but two are quite clear. First, we had assumed that progressive Christian ideas are inherently persuasive. Second, and for that very reason, we also assumed that the triumph of progressive ideas is pretty much inevitable, at least in the Church and in that portion of society that is more or less culturally Christian. We could not believe that others would not recognize the inherent validity and worth of our enlightened and redemptive understanding of the Christian gospel.

Neither of our assumptions is true. It is mistaken—and arrogant—to think that progressive versions of the Christian faith are inherently persuasive. Religious claims, including ours, are never self-evidently true. It is equally mistaken—and dangerous—to assume that progressive Christian ideas will triumph inevitably. The progressive Christian witness will be taken seriously, and make a healing difference, only when and where it is effectively espoused by committed, reflective people who understand that witness, express it compellingly, and enact it together with informed intentionality.

This book seeks to contribute to one of the things now needed—a systematic understanding of progressive Christian beliefs and the reasons for them. This is by no means all that must happen to make the progressive gospel effective in our nation. It may not even be the most important thing needed now. But it *is* important and it *is* needed *now*. It is absolutely urgent that progressive Christians become articulate about the transforming faith that is within them. For the sake of our nation as well as the Church, we must be able to say *what* we believe, and *why*, and to say so effectively.

It is the profoundly healing voice of the Christian faith that is important now, not the specific label we give it. And, in fact, there are at least three reasons for hesitating to refer to the voice now needed as a "progressive" Christian voice. First, "progress" is not always good and continuing the past is not always bad.

Second, the various "progressive" movements and eras in the United States have been political in character and, though not without merit, they have left a great deal to be desired from a Christian standpoint. Finally, unlike our intention here, in current political discourse the term "progressive" is virtually synonymous with, if not a cover for, the term "liberal."

Despite these important concerns, the label "progressive" Christian is retained in this book, partly because the best alternatives are also problematic. For example, to call it "prophetic" Christianity, as some have urged, seems more than a bit presumptuous. Whether a particular Christian voice deserves to be called "prophetic" should be left for history to decide. "Evangelical liberalism," another alternative, seems inadequate, too. It is not a combination of the two traditions but their mutual transformation that is needed. Admittedly, however, the main reason for using "progressive Christianity" here is simply the fact that it is the term now used most often to refer to this Christian viewpoint. Sometimes it is best to accept an imperfect label and endeavor to give it a specific meaning, trusting that it will then be heard and judged fairly for what it is.

In the end labels should not determine our judgments about any point of view, Christian or otherwise. "Conservative" and "liberal" are not inherently wrong standpoints. Isn't every person, including every Christian, in some respects "conserving" of the past and in others "liberated" from it? And surely every faithful Christian voice conveys "good news" and thus is in that sense "evangelical." The issue is not the label; it is the message. To the extent that this book preserves what, of the Christian tradition, should be retained and frees itself from what should be left behind, it might come to the reader as truly good news. And if so, it might also contribute to the kind of "progress" we desperately need today, in the Church, in the country, in the world.

Chapter 1

What Progressive Christianity Is Not

Something new is afoot in Christianity. It is a thought-ful, vital faith offering hope for the Church and the world. Most commonly it is referred to as "progressive Christianity." All of a sudden, especially in the United States, there are progressive Christian websites and e-newsletters, progressive Christian bloggers and discussion boards, progressive Christian periodicals, conferences on progressive Christianity, churches and new organizations arising that claim to present a progressive Christian gospel, and, of course, there are now millions of Christians who identify themselves in this way.

What is progressive Christianity?

The easiest answer, though insufficient, is to say what it is not. Let's begin there, clearing up immediately some possible misconceptions about the progressive Christian perspective.

Not Only Rejecting the Religious Right

Progressive Christians vigorously distinguish themselves from right-wing Christianity. Check out the postings in cyberspace, for example, and you'll find self-identified progressives commonly describing themselves as Christians who emphatically reject the views of Pat Robertson, Jerry Falwell, and Jim Dobson.

This widespread rejection is important. During the past two or three decades these three pillars of the religious right and their followers and funders have managed somehow (lots of money and organizational savvy were a big part of it) to co-opt the name, language, and morals of the Christian faith. They convinced the public that theirs is the true Christian point of view, and then they tried to impose their views on everyone else. America is, or should be, or was supposed to have been, a Christian nation, the right-wingers claimed, and for the benefit of the rest of us they established themselves as the arbiters of what is and is not Christian. So they sought to use the courts and legislatures at every level of government to put into law their views, especially on anything having to do with marriage, sex, and reproduction.

Progressive Christians are saying "No!" They reject the right-wingers' claims for good historical and political reasons. America was not founded as a Christian nation, which fact is all the more remarkable because its founders were Christians. The founders were careful to acknowledge the power of religion in society and to protect the free expression of religion. But the principles on which the country was founded were not those of a specific religion or, for that matter, of religion itself in some general sense. Progressive Christians therefore oppose the agenda of the Christian right-wing because, in part at least, it is historically and politically inaccurate. (They also reject it for Christian reasons, as we shall see.) America is a democracy. Relative to religion this means at a minimum that no one religion or view of religion, including its rejection, is to be privileged over any other.

This negative way of defining progressive Christianity, as I say, is important. But it is not enough. After all, there are a number—a rapidly growing number, thankfully—of conservative or evangelical Christians who also reject the Christian right wing, both its views and its tactics. For example, Gregory Boyd, a leading evangelical mega-church pastor, recently said the right-wingers are, in biblical terms, guilty of the sin of "idolatry" because they assume theirs to be the only defensible interpretation of Christianity and they then conflate it with a particular political viewpoint.[1] They give religious reverence to a political philosophy—or, to be perfectly blunt, they equate Christianity with the socially conservative wing of the Republican Party.

You can be a Republican and a Christian—indeed, you can be a very conservative Republican and a Christian!—and still see that this conflation is a dangerous mistake, both politically and religiously. You don't have to be a progressive Christian to identify and condemn the idolatry of the Christian right wing. Progressive Christianity, in other words, has to be more than a rejection of right-wing Christianity. But what is this "more"?

Not Liberal Christianity in Disguise

Progressive Christians often define themselves against liberal Christianity—and, as we shall see, against conservative Christianity, too. This distinction gets a little fuzzy. Clearly, both are still developing historical movements with considerable internal variety, and both contribute something of importance that progressive Christians wish to affirm and continue.

Still, the distinction is helpful. At the very least the progressive Christian movement today is an effort to criticize and transform the liberal and conservative traditions of American Christianity.

When liberal Christianity emerged in the United States during the middle third of the eighteenth century it was often called "the new theology." Its defining viewpoint was expressed succinctly in a statement by Charles A. Briggs: "The Bible gives us the material for all ages, and leaves to [us] the noble task of shaping the material so as to suit the wants of [our] own time." Making the biblical tradition relevant to the needs of the day—that was the driving passion of liberalism. But how are the legitimate wants or needs of a time to be determined, and according to what criteria do Christians go about shaping the biblical material so as to make its message relevant? To determine the needs of the time liberals counted especially on the democratic process, particularly as its outcomes were interpreted by the newly emerging social sciences. And the criteria on which liberals relied to study and reconstruct the biblical materials were also those of the secular sciences, namely reasoned inquiry based on empirical evidence. The liberal interpretation of the Christian message was to be consistent with reason and experience.[2]

A progressive Christian perspective, we shall see, does not minimize the Christian mandate to make the gospel relevant in each new age, and it does not object to the sciences, democracy, empirical evidence, and certainly not to reasoned inquiry. In those respects, progressive Christianity unabashedly continues the liberal Christian outlook. However, the liberals went wrong, from a progressive perspective, when reasoning based on (supposedly common) human experience became for them more than valued *tools and tests* to be utilized in shaping the inherited Christian materials; gradually it became also the *source* of liberal theology. As that happened, the "material" of historic Christian faith—its stories, symbols, ideas, analyses, and imperatives—moved to the dim and largely optional margins of liberal Christian reflection. Liberal theology became something more akin to a philosophy of religion.

Philosophy is not at all a bad thing, of course. But what of the distinctive insights offered in the Scriptures and historic Christian reflection? Is there nothing of value in Christian understandings of creation, humanity, freedom, sin, hope, healing, history, and the meaning of life? Do these offer no critical edge, no distinctive perspectives worth introducing and developing as a Christian contribution to the contemporary search for truth?

The liberal failure to keep the distinctive resources of the Christian inheritance at the center of their reflection was rooted in another failure, one common to the late nineteenth and early twentieth centuries. Liberals "forgot" that our human beliefs and practices, individually and collectively, are fed and formed by our distinctive human histories. In other words, the liberals were seduced by "modernism." Modernism is the idea that there is one truth grounded in the nature of things in such a way that thinking individuals can have immediate access to this truth through reasoned analysis of contemporary experience, without any special dependence on inherited resources. It is the idea that we don't need history in the pursuit of truth; we can go right to the truth by thinking clearly now. The point is not that "history is bunk," as Henry Ford once claimed. Rather it is that our varied histories, traditions, ancient texts, and the like have no special role in guiding and testing contemporary life.

Gradually moving toward this point of view, liberal Christianity too often became—by the 1940s and 1950s—little more than the sanctimonious expression of common beliefs and values. Liberal sermons became secular social commentary that began with a Scripture and ended with prayer. Liberal Christian education became secular schooling interlaced with sentimental renditions of stories from the Bible. Liberal Christian morality was reduced to the common cultural interpretation of rectitude. Like almost everyone else in that time, liberal Christians forgot the importance of the past, their specifically Christian past—their rich biblical and historical inheritance.

Like *almost* everyone else, but not everyone! Not conservative Christians. To be conservative means to conserve a heritage. Conservative Christians, against the majority of the culture and, indeed, also against much of the Church, retained a sense of the special importance of Christian history for Christian people. In that respect, progressive Christianity allies itself with Christian conservatism. But not entirely, by any means, as we shall see.

Not Conservative Christianity Polished Up

Since the middle of the nineteenth century, conservative Christianity in America has tended in one of two directions. One emphasized right action, the other right belief. Neither totally dismissed the other's concern, to be sure, but their different emphases led nevertheless to quite different forms of conservative Christian piety. The focus on right belief was especially indebted to the great sixteenth-century theologian John Calvin. In America, however, its most influential intellectual shaping came through the scholarly "fundamentalism" of the Princeton theologians in the late 1800s, a school of thought to which we shall return shortly.

The emphasis on right action in nineteenth-century conservatism was motivated in large part by the active piety of John Wesley, an Anglican priest who founded Methodism a century earlier, even if it spread well beyond the confines of the Wesleyan movement and its theology. Its blossoming in the middle of the nineteenth century is often called the Second Great Awakening. Its message was a call for personal and social "holiness," that is, for personal discipline coupled with the vigorous pursuit of a just social order. The term "evangelicalism" is an apt designation of this emphasis, and it is a form of conservatism that the evangelicals of today would do well to emulate more fully.

The nineteenth-century evangelicals—represented, for example, by the "hellfire and brimstone" revival preacher Charles G. Finney—were zealots in the movements to abolish slavery, establish women's rights, and overcome poverty. Finney and like-minded evangelicals denounced the mainline preachers for their moral timidity—or as one of them (Theodore Weld) said, for their "truckling subserviency to power . . . clinging with mendicant sycophancy to the skirts of wealth and influence . . . [and] cowering before bold transgression when it stalks among the high places of power with fashion in its train. . . ."[3] Evangelical couples in their wedding vows renounced the rule of husband over wife sanctioned by civil law. About the same time, evangelical groups like the Wesleyan Methodists, Free Methodists, Church of the Nazarene, and Christian and Missionary Alliance came into being in order to minister to the poor who, they said, were demeaned by establishment churches and "oppressed" (their term) by the "rich and powerful."

The strong witness of the evangelical conservatives flourished until the Civil War. In the immense social strife after that war, however, their concerns turned sharply inward and private. By the 1870s evangelicalism was no longer preaching "social holiness." Now the focus was on personal piety, which increasingly became trivialized as abstinence from card-playing, smoking, drinking, dancing, and other "sins of the flesh."

Why the tragic retreat from a full-bodied Christian witness? The answer in large part, I think, was the absence of a full-bodied theology, a theology adequate to guide and sustain the evangelical spirit when it encountered the recalcitrance of social injustice. In other words, its heart was not nourished by the head; it "conserved" an evangelical spirit but not a credible belief system to support that spirit. In a manner analogous to the later decline of liberalism (which, interestingly, was also debilitated by a war, World War I), evangelical conservatism became little more than the baptized mores of its populist and conservative social order.

The other form of American conservatism rising to prominence after the Civil War is best represented by the "fundamentalism" of the Princeton School. How ironic that today this term connotes anti-intellectualism. Exactly the opposite was true of the Princeton fundamentalists in the 1880s and '90s. They were stalwart intellectuals who endeavored to validate the claims of the Christian faith intellectually. Scholars like A. A. Hodge and B. B. Warfield sought to do so by grounding Christian beliefs in what they said was the unique character of the Bible, its "inerrancy." They debated their views of Scripture openly, paid attention to new biblical scholarship without fear, and revised their views on the Bible when the evidence required it. In fact, based on their own biblical study, they eventually concluded that the term "inerrancy" could apply only to the original manuscripts of the Bible, now lost. Therefore any contradictions in Scripture (such as the two different stories in Genesis 1 and 2) came about through human error that crept in later while copying and recopying the original documents. Obviously, if the original manuscripts were lost, the claim that they were without error could not be challenged. The unique character of the "original autographs" was therefore protected, but at great cost—they were not available to guide subsequent Christians' life and thought. The fundamentalist insistence on biblical inerrancy was thus untenable, if applied to the current Bible, or inapplicable, if applied to Scripture in its earliest form. In time, fundamentalism could only continue as an anti-intellectual mass movement wedded to a rhetoric of biblical inerrancy that no reasonable study of Scripture could sustain.

A progressive Christian theology shares the nineteenth-century evangelicals' commitment to social justice (even though in retrospect their views were naïve regarding issues of race, gender, sexuality, and even class). But a theology that can endure must be much more deliberate than that of the evangelicals in its intellectual awareness and articulation. The mind is not all of human nature by any means, but it is part of and essential to a healthy humanity. Similarly, a full and credible theology is essential to a healthy Christianity. Hence a progressive Christian movement, if it is to be more than a fad, must be resolutely theological as well as active in the pursuit of justice.

In this respect the model of the nineteenth-century fundamentalists is strangely—perhaps shockingly—to be respected by progressive Christians today because the early fundamentalists certainly used their minds. Eventually, though, the fundamentalist movement let a dogma about the Bible obscure the truth about the Bible and thus, too, the nature of biblical truth and biblical authority. That failing continues today in much of conservative Christianity. Conserving the Bible *as it is* is one thing; conserving the Bible as conservative dogmatists *imagine it to be* is another. The Bible is not inerrant, in history, science, and ethics—nor is it inerrant in theology. And, as we shall see, it does not need to be in order to ground, guide, and sustain Christian identity.

What, then, do progressive Christians learn from conservatives? They learn the very thing that liberal Christianity forgot—that all people, including Christians, are historical people. We are formed by our past. More than that, as Christians we live today, fully in the present, drawing from that past. The Bible, and the tradition of debate, disagreement, reflection, correction, and innovation that stems from the Bible, is the distinctively Christian contribution that we bring—as one set of voices among politically equal others—to our contemporary public discussions about what is true and good.

How do we dare bring into our current debates the resources of a tradition that is multiple and fallible, and grounded in an ancient text that is fallible and diverse? Because that text and the traditions it forms, in which our identity is grounded, model precisely that kind of dialogue. More than that, this text and the traditions it forms mandate for us, as an act of personal faith, this kind of contribution to the public debates we are now having.

To pretend that our histories are absolute or inerrant is a mistake, but to ignore the power of our fallible traditions to inform, enrich, criticize, and transform the present is a grave mistake, too. In fact, we are historically formed, and from our histories we live in the present. To live today—knowledgably, reflectively, self-critically—bringing into our time the redemptive resources of biblical reflection and practice is to be a progressive Christian.

Then What Are We?

Progressive Christianity is an analysis and rejection, in the name of Christian faith, of the message that comes from right-wing Christianity. But it is more than that. It is also a critique of liberal and conservative Christianity, as well as a continuation of valuable elements provided by each. But what, more fully, is it that progressive Christians affirm, and why?

The remainder of this small volume describes basic progressive Christian beliefs. Or, more precisely, it describes one progressive Christian belief perspective.

There is room in the progressive Christian community for differences. In fact, some progressive Christians may disagree about the choice of basic topics that form the structure of this book. And there is certainly reason for progressive believers to differ within these basic topics, emphasizing one point rather than another or adding something that they think has been missed in this discussion. All of that is as it should be in a theological discussion.

"Theological," you say in surprise, "I thought this was about what real people believe." You are right, that's what this book is about: what real progressive Christians believe, and why. But that is precisely what theology is about in progressive Christianity today and, indeed, in much of the Christian tradition. Theology is exploring what is believed, and why; it is trying to make those beliefs clear, to test them, and to identify the good reasons (if there are some!) for holding them.

What are "good reasons" for a belief?

As you will see, for the progressive Christian they are not reasons that are merely personally satisfying or only satisfying to those who share the belief. Progressive Christianity is not a "you just have to believe it" point of view. But neither, for us, are good reasons the same as "proofs." They are not the kind of argument the conclusion of which any reasonable person will necessarily accept if he or she understands the argument. Good reasons don't force assent.

I will put it this way: "Good reasons" are reasons for believing something that a person who does not share that belief can nevertheless respect. They are reasons that someone else thinks to be credible even if they are not compelling for him or her.

This introductory volume describes a progressive Christian perspective and the good reasons for holding this point of view. But it seeks to do more than that. It seeks to explain why this credible, if not provable, point of view is worth organizing one's life around and giving one's life to. Not blindly (that's forbidden by the view point, as you will see) and not without a willingness to change (that willingness is something progressive Christianity requires). But a perspective worth entering and living by.

In other words, this book seeks to say why progressive Christianity is "gospel," a word of "good news" that merits living for and sharing with others. And "others" includes liberals who are searching, conservatives who are open, and others who are curious.

POINTS FOR REFLECTION

- Liberal Christians held that the Bible provides the material relevant for all ages, and calls each generation to reshape those biblical insights and convictions for its time, based on reason and experience.

- Liberal Christianity too often became little more than the sanctimonious expression of common cultural beliefs and values.

- Early "evangelicals" coupled personal holiness with the pursuit of justice. Their leaders condemned slavery, challenged the inequities of capitalism, and championed the rights of women.

- Evangelicalism no longer preached "social holiness." Now its focus was exclusively on abstinence from "sins of the flesh."

- The Princeton "fundamentalists" gradually concluded that "inerrancy" applied only to the first (now lost) manuscripts of the Bible.

- Eventually the fundamentalist movement let a dogma about the Bible obscure the truth about the Bible and thus, too, the nature of biblical truth and biblical authority.

- A progressive Christian movement, if it is to be more than a fad, must be resolutely theological as well as active in the pursuit of justice.

- To pretend that our past histories are absolute or inerrant is a mistake, but to ignore the power of our fallible traditions to transform the present is also a grave mistake.

Chapter 2
Bible:
Negotiating the Heritage

Christianity did not begin with the Bible. It began with Jesus of Nazareth as he was understood and proclaimed by his followers. But we must begin with the Bible for at least two reasons. First, it is the source of what is known about Jesus as interpreted by those who believed in him. Therefore, for historical reasons, we must start with the Bible.

Second, the Bible—or at least our divergent understandings of it—is the source of basic disagreements among Christians, as evidenced by the sharp controversies in the mainline denominations today regarding homosexuality. Divergent understandings of the Bible also relate to differences between Christians and some of Christianity's sharpest critics, such as atheists Sam Harris in *Letter to a Christian Nation* and Richard Dawkins in *The God Delusion*. For these reasons too, then, we need to begin with a consideration of the Bible, its nature, and its proper role in Christian thought and practice.

Being Biblical about the Bible

It is silly to claim, as some cynics do, that the Bible can be made to say anything. A serious comparison of the Bible with the Scriptures of the great Eastern religions, for example, makes it clear that each is distinctive and, though they may share some commonalities, none can be twisted into a replica of another. The Bible, like sacred texts generally, has a distinctive if complex perspective on the world and how life is to be lived in it.

But it is also impossible to claim, responsibly, that what the Bible says is without error. The Bible is not inerrant. This is so clearly evident that we are tempted to dismiss its denial out of hand. We must dismiss it, of course, but the doctrine of biblical inerrancy has an origin that might be instructive for us, even today.

The view that the Bible is free from error is not a historic Christian doctrine. Of course the great theologians of the Church did claim that the Bible has a unique and exceptional character, even using a term like "infallible" to refer to the reliability of the Bible as a guide to truth. But when these same theologians, such as Augustine or Luther, went on soundly to condemn certain books, sections, or concepts in the Bible, we immediately are warned that by terms like "infallible" they could not have meant being "without error."

The use of "inerrancy" as a way of affirming the Bible's unique character was developed systematically in the seventeenth century as the basis of the Protestant reaction to the Roman Catholic claim for the inerrancy of the Church. And both doctrines—"dogmas" really—began to be qualified almost from the start. But the qualifications were never sufficient to adapt the doctrines to the evidence. The Catholic understanding of tradition, of which the Bible is the foundation, offers much from which Protestants can and should learn. Nevertheless, the notion that any element of tradition, however carefully circumscribed and defined, is or even could be uniquely protected from error is simply false and dangerous in the extreme. The temptation in some sectors of Protestantism to say that the Bible is protected from error is no less dangerous and no less false. Both lead to arrogance and bigotry, and both flatly contradict the facts.

It is now common, even among some more conservative or "evangelical" Protestant theologians, to acknowledge the contradictions in Scripture, which means Scripture's errors.[4] For example, Matthew 19 and Luke 16 disagree with Mark 10 on the grounds for divorce. One account must be wrong. Matthew 20 and Mark 10 differ on who requested special treatment for the Sons of Zebedee. Both cannot be right. Matthew 27 and Mark 15 differ with Luke 23 about what the centurion said when the Temple was torn in two. Was it "Truly this man was God's son!" or "Certainly this man was innocent"? One report has to be wrong. Mark 10, Matthew 20, and Luke 18 are each different regarding the number and location of the blind men whom Jesus healed at Jericho. Mark 16 says the women who visited the empty tomb left and said nothing to anyone, but Matthew and Luke offer very different accounts. When the rich young ruler addressed Jesus as "good teacher," the reply reported in Mark and Luke is: "Why do you call me good? Only God is good." But the reply reported by Matthew is significantly different: "Why do you ask me what is good?"

If being biblical means speaking about the Bible in a manner that is consistent with the Bible, then the doctrine of inerrancy is unbiblical.

But the issue is not simply textual errors. If we are to be biblical about the Bible, the change that Matthew introduced into this story of the rich young ruler suggests something far more important than errors of fact for us to consider. Mark and Luke do not feel compelled to ascribe God-like goodness to Jesus. But, given his different theological perspective, Matthew does. He cannot allow Jesus to admit such a radical difference between himself and God. So Matthew changes the question asked in order to change the answer Jesus gives. Here we begin to see that there are not only conflicting factual accounts in the Bible; there are also different and conflicting theologies!

This theological diversity applies even to the most central elements of Christian faith—understandings of Jesus and salvation. Consider, for example, the Four Gospels: In Mark, the earliest gospel, Jesus is proclaimed as a preacher who is adopted by God at the moment of his baptism, and salvation is offered to those who, following the example of Jesus, are faithful throughout their suffering until the coming of the reign of God. In Matthew, however, Jesus is God's son from the moment of Mary's conception, and salvation comes through obedience to the New Torah, the new Jewish Law. Luke agrees with Matthew about the beginning of Jesus' sonship, but proclaims salvation as the divine reign that is coming in a future history. For John, the last gospel, Jesus' special status predates his baptism, even his birth: "In the beginning was the Word, and the Word was with God, and the Word was God." For John, Jesus is the pre-existent Logos (or creative structure of the world) made flesh, and salvation is "abundant life," a kind of mystic oneness that is available to believers already in the here and now.

Theological diversity is evident throughout the Bible. Views of human relationships that are authoritarian and liberationist, hierarchical and egalitarian, are all found there. In the New Testament the Jewish Torah is said to be abrogated by Christ at some points and fulfilled by Christ at others. The equality of women is supported in the Bible, as is their subordination to men. Salvation is by faith in Jesus in some portions of the New Testament but in others it is independent of any such faith.

We may disagree somewhat about the understandings of the gospel presented in the varied New Testament writings. But if we are willing to let these texts speak for themselves, we will agree that they, the documents at the foundation of Christianity, do present varying theologies. They offer different understandings of Christianity—often complementary, sometimes competing, but different. To deny this diversity is unbiblical.

"Well," one hears the reaction, "so much for biblical authority!"

This is an understandable reaction. How can a Scripture containing such diverse views be authoritative for Christian faith? Let's think about that question, which means at the same time thinking again about "authority."

Thinking about Biblical Authority

It is often assumed that if the Bible is "authoritative" for Christians, then throughout the ages Christians must conform to its message.

But why give place of privilege to such a book? A writing from so long ago and from such a different cultural history might be interesting to us today, even, perhaps, instructive in many respects. After all, we do learn from other times and places. But why should it be authoritative? Add to this the morally despicable views expressed in the Bible—rebellious sons are to be stoned (Deuteronomy 13), virgins are to be taken in war and the other women killed (Numbers 31), slaves are to work extra hard if the owner is a Christian (1 Timothy 6), and wives are to be silent in church (1 Corinthians 14)—and the question of biblical authority is forcefully underscored.

Even these considerations, however, are less decisive than the conundrum that arises when we take seriously the obvious theological diversity of the Bible. The Bible is full of different theological (and ethical) views. It simply cannot be conformed to! The authority of the Bible, if it means anything at all, cannot require conforming to this complex of different, sometimes contradictory, points of view.

Some years ago I read a short essay on "authority" by Hannah Arendt.[5] It offers a historical account of what I would call the "normative" view of authority, the view that an authority is a singular standard or norm to which everyone should conform. Arendt found the origins of this concept in the development of centralized political rule among the ancient Greeks. What could be the foundation of such a rule? The Greeks debated this matter and resolved it in different ways, but the Romans, who came later, gave it a definitive answer. What can be the foundation of Roman rule? Well, of course, the foundation of Rome itself!

"At the heart of Roman politics," Arendt says, "stands the conviction of the sacredness of foundation, in the sense that once something has been founded it remains binding for all future generations." In Rome "religion meant *religare*: to be tied back, obligated . . . to the legendary effort to lay the foundations, to build the cornerstone, to found for eternity. To be religious meant to be tied to the past." Arendt adds: "The word *auctoritas* derives from the verb '[to] augment,'" and what is augmented is "the foundation." With the Romans, this legendary foundation gradually was transmuted into a canon, a standard of measurements and rules applicable to all behaviors and beliefs, including those of religion.

Early institutional Christianity understandably appropriated this Roman view of authority: An authority is a uniform standard to which all under it must conform. The Apostles, witnesses to Jesus, became the "founding fathers" of the Church. The Church derived its authority from the apostolic witness so long as it conformed to that witness. The dispute among Christians at the time of the Reformation was among Romanized Christians. Although they came to different conclusions, Protestants and Catholics alike worked with a Roman or normative interpretation of Christianity's founding event, now transmuted into a biblical canon. At the level of doctrine, the Bible was said to be, or to provide, an objective measure to be conformed to, and acknowledging its authority meant accepting the obligation to conform to it.

This Roman view of authority is very different from the view at work in the world that gave rise to the Hebrew Bible (Old Testament). In this world each generation treated its authoritative past with respect, and with creativity! The prophets, for example, lived from their histories, but they did so innovatively—adapting and sometimes even reversing past interpretations of the exodus or the wilderness experience in order to meet the needs of new times. James Sanders, a biblical scholar, has argued that after the Exile, Hebraic "theologians" removed the story of the conquest of Canaan from what came to be known as the Pentateuch, their fundamental authoritative source.[6] They decided to end the Torah with the book of Deuteronomy, not Joshua, because the centrality of the "promised land" no longer worked for them far away in Babylonian captivity.

In the Hebraic traditions, creativity rather than conformity was at work. Tradition was authoritative, but not as a fixed and singular past that must be replicated. Authority did not mean that which "authorizes" by virtue of being conformed to. It meant something else. What?

The concept of "authority" is complex in the New Testament, but one meaning is particularly interesting for addressing the question at hand. Jesus, for example, is said to have spoken to the crowds as one having "authority," *exousia* (Mark 1:22, Luke 4:32, and Matthew 7:29). Basic to the uses of *exousia* in these passages is the notion of a right and power to act or respond creatively.[7] This power is first of all God's, then Jesus', and finally it is extended to the believing community. The focus is on the creativity, power, and freedom of the authoritative source. That is, authority has to do with the creativity appropriate to an action, not the conformity appropriate to a reaction. In fact, authority extends authority—extends the rightful freedom and power to respond creatively. Authority does not command conformity; it commends freedom.

Authority viewed in this way is not an "authorizer," something that specifies unyielding standards to which one must conform. Authority is formative, not normative. Authority is empowerment.

Interestingly, this alternative view of authority is preserved for us in the English word "author." An authority in this alternative is that which authors—that which gives being to, forms, empowers, calls to creativity. Even literal authors testify to the fact that their creations, their characters, take on a vitality of their own. The author gives life to the characters, but these creations are not mere puppets; they take on a life of their own so that in a secondary sense at least they begin to author themselves. They acquire a measure of autonomy, of self-creation. They even contend against the author who continues to "write" them, taking the plot in directions unanticipated by the one who gave and continues to give them life.

The author, giving life, bestows freedom; the creatures, given life, become creative. And the creativity of the character continues . . . so long as it remains rooted in the undergirding power of the writer. Indeed, the being and identity of the character is dependent on its interaction with the being and identity of the author. The character cannot be who it is without remaining grounded in the author, but for the character to be authored or created at all is for it also to be creative.

Using the Bible Biblically

The Bible is authoritative for progressive Christians because it empowers, not because it confines. The Bible is heeded because it forms us, not because it norms us. We read its stories, we listen to its parables, we hear its admonitions, we follow its reasoning, we are taught by its conclusions. In our personal lives and in our corporate worship, the Bible is the source out of which we live self-consciously as Christians, as we live into new times, confront new challenges, and address new issues. It authors our Christian identity.

The diversity of viewpoints within the Bible, even on important theological matters, does not undermine its authority. On the contrary, it is essential to biblical authority. It is a means through which the Bible teaches us to think for ourselves, to work out our own identity as Christians in new cultures. Biblical diversity is one of the means through which, we believe, the Spirit of God provokes and inspires us, nourishes and forms us. The very diversity of voices in Scripture empowers us. Therefore, we live continuously in relation to the biblical text because we experience it, with all its richness, as our formative foundation, the continuing source of our dynamic Christian self-understanding.

Like the writers within the text, we are always taught by our sacred past, and like them we are often chastened and corrected by it. As we shall see in later chapters, among the diverse voices of Scripture are those that critique our individualistic notions of salvation, condemn our indifference to the rest of creation, challenge our imprisoning "free" market assumptions, unmask our shallow views of responsibility, dismantle our notions of rank and power, denounce our religious and national exceptionalism, and reject the contrived categories by which we divide humankind . . . among other unsettling things. We are empowered by the diverse voices of Scripture to decide for ourselves how we shall respond to these sharp challenges, to be sure, but as Christians we cannot avoid wrestling with them.

And sometimes, like the biblical writers themselves, we dare to take views that differ from voices in the Bible. We do so reverently and thoughtfully, continuing to listen to the critical dialogue inside and outside our religious communities. But in fact we do disagree with biblical teachings. We permit divorce, although the Bible rejects it. We pay and charge interest, although the Bible condemns it. We reject slavery even when the master is kind and monarchy even when the ruler is benevolent, although the Bible endorses both. And we condemn patriarchy, despite the fact that patriarchal perspectives are much stronger in the Bible than egalitarian ones. We are bold to take these positions, however, not despite the Bible but because we believe that its rich dialogue—its continuing negotiation with the tradition that it inherited—has empowered us to do so. We live in relation to our sacred Scripture—listening, learning, and sometimes "talking back."

Our distinctive identity as Christians emerges and is sustained and transformed as we engage this text. We read its stories and are empowered to write new ones, stories drawn from our own time and place. We listen to its parables and explore new endings, sometimes with startling insights. We attend to its dominant voices but then listen attentively, trying to catch the silent words of those whom the recorders left out. We follow the reasoning of the dominant voices—Paul and the theologians behind the Gospels. We listen to them and we agree, or modify, or sometimes sharply disagree. They are good teachers, the kind who help us think for ourselves in our times and cultures.

The Bible is not our authority in the sense of legalistically mandating conformity to its every teaching. The Bible is the progressive Christian's authority because in our engagement with it we are authored as Christians. In its rich, dynamic, provocative, and empowering diversity, it is the continuing source of our Christian identity. Reflecting the *exousia* of Jesus, it grants us freedom, grounds our creativity, guides our thinking, challenges our conclusions, inspires our hearts, and thus it empowers us—in conversation with our contemporary communities—to act responsibly as citizens of the world.

POINTS FOR REFLECTION

- The claim that tradition can be protected from error is false and dangerous. The belief that the Bible is free from error is no less so. Both lead to arrogance and bigotry, and both contradict the facts.

- There are not only conflicting factual accounts in the Bible, there are also different and sometimes conflicting theologies, even with respect to Jesus and salvation.

- How can a Scripture containing diverse theological views be authoritative? Add to this the morally despicable views in the Bible and the question is forcefully underscored. What does biblical "authority" mean?

- The dominant concept of "authority" in the New Testament has to do with the right and power to act creativity. Biblical authority does not command conformity, it commends freedom. It is formative, not normative—it is empowerment.

- The diversity of viewpoints in the Bible does not undermine its authority. It is a means through which the Bible teaches us to think for ourselves as Christians in new circumstances.

- Among the voices of Scripture are those that critique our individualistic notions of salvation, condemn our indifference to the rest of creation, challenge our "free" market assumptions, and denounce our religious and national exceptionalism.

- We are empowered by the diverse voices of Scripture to decide for ourselves how we shall respond to their sharp challenges, but as Christians we cannot avoid wrestling with them.

- The Bible is our authority because in our engagement with it we are authored as Christians. It grants us freedom, guides our thinking, challenges our conclusions, and empowers us to act responsibly as citizens of the world.

Chapter 3
Christ:
Overturning the Categories

Progressive Christian reflection begins with Jesus Christ for one quite understandable reason: it seeks to take history seriously.

Human beings are historical beings. We all stand in traditions of inheritance. Indeed, we stand in more than one such tradition. We are people of particular nations, particular regions of those nations, particular racial/ethnic heritages, particular family traditions, and so on. In each of these streams of inheritance we imbibe distinctive constellations of feelings, values, practices, and concepts flowing from the past. That is no less true of Christians. Our specifically Christian identity is derived from the long, complex, and dynamic Jesus tradition. Who we are as Christians arises from our personal and historical connection with Jesus Christ.

What does that mean?

Beginning with Jesus

Beginning with Jesus Christ means that we start, not with history, but with the witness of his first followers to the significance of Jesus. The New Testament is not a history, although it contains significant elements of history. It is an interpretation of a historical figure, Jesus of Nazareth, provided by those whose lives he had transformed. Their encounter with Jesus had turned upside down the categories through which they understood themselves and their world. They were transformed. The New Testament is an interpretation of Jesus—or, more precisely, a collection of interpretations—that seeks to explain and proclaim the significance of Jesus.

The earliest explanations spoke primarily about what had happened in and through Jesus. "What has been accomplished because of Jesus?" The answers given were varied because Jesus was experienced differently by different followers. As time passed, however, his followers began to ask another, more speculative, question; one about the nature of Jesus. "What must Jesus have been like—or what must Jesus be like—in order for this change to have happened?" Again, different experiences and, increasingly, the varying cultural and social resources of his followers gave rise to varied answers. Jewish and Hellenistic, poor and middle class, persecuted and secure, urban and rural—people responded to and interpreted Jesus of Nazareth through the lenses of their own cultural experiences. The variety is apparent already in the New Testament. And now that other ancient gospels are coming to light we realize that the early interpretations of Jesus were even more varied than those presented in the New Testament.

This diversity is not a problem. It is, first, a great reservoir of resources to enrich, provoke, and challenge our own interpretations of Jesus. We should maintain that reservoir with its manifold understandings; we should not hastily drain it. We should not say, for example, that the earliest witnesses are, simply for that reason, to be preferred. Why should they be? Of course, if we are seeking clues to the *history* behind the first interpretations of Jesus of Nazareth, then the earliest layers of New Testament literature may be the more useful resources. But getting at the history, even if that can be done, is not the same as getting at its meaning for us. In any case, the earliest meanings given to a historical event are never exhaustive, nor usually are they to be preferred. For example, were the first interpretations of September 11 the only or best interpretations of what happened that day? Insights can grow and deepen with time, just as they can also distract or diminish. The whole range of New Testament testimonies to Jesus' significance should be retained as a reminder of the multiple ways that Jesus can be understood and, perhaps, even as a guide to the possibilities for us today.

Secondly, however, the varied interpretations of Jesus call us to take a stand. Each of the interpretations is just that, one interpretation. It is a particular standpoint, one bold witness to the significance of Jesus. Each is a specific answer to the question, what does Jesus mean for us in our time?

It will not do for progressive Christians to be any less specific today about the meaning of Jesus, even if we differ among ourselves as did those first Christians. What does Jesus mean for us today? In the answer to that question lies the foundation of our Christian identity and the core of our individual witness in the world. Our answers should be accepting of alternatives, but also critical of them as well as self-critical, and open to change. The progressive Christian's witness, however, must be clear and compelling if progressive Christianity is again to have a powerful healing voice in the Church and in the world.

The Meaning of Jesus

What does Jesus mean for progressive Christians today? In order to answer this question, I suggest that we take as our guide the Christian councils of the fourth and fifth centuries, those gatherings of bishops and theologians at Nicea, Constantinople, Ephesus, and Chalcedon called to clarify and define the nature and content of Christian faith over and against all rival interpretations.

To many progressive Christians this way of addressing the question will seem unpromising, if not utterly shocking. Few of us think of what came to be known as the "christological" councils—because they debated about the nature of Christ—as being particularly progressive. Indeed, in the history of Christian theology, and still today, their conclusions are often cited in an attempt to reign in supposedly aberrant forms of Christian belief. And that, in fact, was their original purpose, too—to cut back the great flowering of Christian expression in the first few centuries in order to produce the well-pruned tree of "orthodoxy." More than that, the conciliar process was often motivated by political rather than theological interests, conducted via infighting and intrigue, and driven by the needs of empire for unity and control. What could these christological councils contribute to a progressive Christian understanding of Jesus? Let's consider that question.

The councils sought to establish an orthodox framework within which all other interpretations of Jesus, if valid, should fit as elements or parts of its "authoritative" whole. This framework was "incarnationism," the view that God is incarnate in Jesus Christ. This was but one construal of the significance of Jesus in the New Testament, of course, and a late one at that, best articulated by the Gospel of John. But by the fourth century it had gained pre-eminence. The purpose of the councils was to clarify this idea, to say what it did and did not mean. The conclusion of the councils was audacious—a conclusion, I think, that Christianity has not fully assimilated even to this day!

The first council was at Nicea in 325. It was about the relationship of the "Word" or, we might say, the "form of divinity" present in Jesus to the divinity of God himself. A theologian named Arius (who ended up losing the argument) wished, quite admirably, to protect the uniqueness of God's divinity. With that in mind, he insisted that the divinity present in Christ was, so to speak, made by God but it was not one with God's own divinity. It was certainly a divine identity, but a divinity lower than God's. Arius's view was rejected at Nicea: the council concluded that the Word (or divinity) present in Christ was begotten of God, born of God's own substance. The divinity of Jesus was the same as the Father's.

This is arcane language, to be sure, but it is also extraordinary in its meaning. It is saying that the God who is present in Jesus is the "truly true" God, not some lesser form of divinity. It is a rejection of the view that there are higher and lower levels of divinity and that the divinity present in Jesus is not God's. Nicea was adamant: Even if the divinity in Jesus is next to the top, right under God's, that does not suffice. The God present in Jesus is the real and full and true God.

The next council came in 381 at Constantinople. The main question it addressed is a reasonable one: If the divinity present in Jesus is true divinity, how can Jesus' humanity be our kind of humanity? Humanity is intrinsically imperfect, necessarily other than divinity. How can full divinity be present in imperfect men and women? "It cannot," was the reply of many thoughtful Christians. The humanity of Jesus, they said, must have been a unique kind of humanity, perhaps even a pretended humanity, but not humanity as we know it.

No, the council concluded. The full divinity of deity became flesh, became human, exactly as we are. The "truly true" God became one with "truly true" humanity. In Jesus, according to the council, real divinity is at one with real humanity.

Well, is that in fact possible? The controversy continued about what was now a doubly perplexing claim, that real and true divinity is present in real and true humanity. So another half century later, in 431, a third council was convened, in Ephesus. It debated the relationship of the humanity and divinity that prior councils had said characterized Jesus.

The most credible view of this relationship, it seemed to some, was to say that the divinity of God, although "in" Jesus' full humanity, was nevertheless separate from it—enveloped in it, perhaps, as an egg can be in, but separate from, a basket. Jesus was fully divine in intellect but human in all other respects—that was one version of this proposal. Or Jesus had a fully divine soul in an otherwise fully human person—that was another.

No, the council insisted. In Jesus, true divinity is perfectly united with true humanity. Full divinity (not some lesser divinity) and full humanity (not some elevated humanity) are "perfectly united" (not partially so).

The Council of Chalcedon followed twenty years later, in 451, in part to beat back a further effort to moderate the radical incarnationism of previous councils. The Council of Chalcedon rejected that effort. What happened in Jesus, it affirmed, is the full union of full divinity with full humanity.

Why, we must ask, did the christological councils insist on so puzzling a formula? To get at an answer we should ask a prior question: what, theologically, were they attempting to do? The answer is this: they were trying to give unqualified force to the claim that full and complete salvation is made possible in Jesus Christ. Not some lesser salvation, not partial salvation, not salvation for a specialized form of humanity. Their intent was to claim that somehow, in Jesus, fully adequate salvation is fully possible for fully human beings.

But why did the councils settle on this particular formula for making that point? Because they assumed, first, that divinity, whatever else it is or does, is the source of salvation, and, second, that divinity works by somehow becoming one with, joining with, that which it seeks to save. The most succinct expression of this view was Gregory of Nyssa's: "What God has not assumed, God has not saved." It is by becoming one with humanity that God makes our salvation possible. Since the Christian claim is that salvation is possible, then it was necessary for the councils to insist that the true God has truly taken on true humanity.

The Message of the Councils for Today

The point of Christology is the doctrine of the incarnation— the claim that God has become one with humanity. That, put mildly, is an extraordinary assertion. But in fact the doctrine becomes even more extraordinary if we take seriously another basic affirmation in the New Testament. This is the claim, strange to our ears, that salvation is about more than humanity; it is about the world. John says that the purpose of the incarnation is the salvation of the world. "God so loved the world"—that is John's good news. And Paul, in Romans 8, proclaims the coming salvation of not only "we ourselves," but of "the entire created order." The whole creation, Paul says, will be set free from its bondage to decay and death. And why not? If, in the Christian view, God created the world and saw it to be good, should we then be surprised by the claim that God will save the creation, too?

Of course this is not how we are inclined to understand salvation. As modern Westerners we are accustomed to thinking in ways that center first on the individual self, and then on selves collectively, on humanity. The idea that salvation (whatever it may be) might apply to the entire creation seems bizarre. What is strange to us, however, was not strange in the biblical world, as we shall see in a later chapter. The biblical world was a world of connections, among people and between people and their larger natural and symbolic environments. That is why it seemed reasonable to the early followers of Jesus to think of what he had accomplished not simply in personal, but also in cosmic, terms. Salvation had to be conceived comprehensively because the world was conceived as interconnected.

Whatever our response to so robust a view of salvation, its requirements are already implicit in the doctrine of the incarnation, when that doctrine is taken to its logical conclusion. In Jesus of Nazareth we have come to see that God is with us. But not with us only, for God seeks the salvation of the "entire created order." So if God assumes what God seeks to save, then God is somehow incarnate in the entire creation—the ordinary and extraordinary, the broken and the whole, the known and the unknown, the familiar and the mysterious world in all its dimensions. God is not reducible to the world; "God" and "world" are not synonyms. The world is not perfect. But God's place is this imperfect place, and its destiny and God's are joined. God is with us, and the "us" includes all creation.

The Gospel of John expresses this by saying that God is one with the world as its "logos" or "organizational structure." This logos, present everywhere, is revealed to us in Jesus of Nazareth. In the history of Christian reflection, the oneness of creator and creation, the divine and the non-divine, has been conceived in varied ways, always seeking, as John did, to use the concepts of the day to attempt to make the point. Progressive Christians today may choose to think about this God/world relationship anew, using modern resources. That topic will be addressed in the next chapter.

For now the proposal is simply this: that we ground our progressive Christian vision in the bold good news of the christological councils, taken to its logical conclusion. The divine is at one with the cosmos and all that is in it. God is in and with the world. God is with us and the rest of creation, too—fully God, fully world, fully one.

Some Consequences of a Progressive Christology

What does the doctrine of the incarnation mean, concretely, for a progressive Christian understanding? The remainder of this book is an effort to contribute to the development of an answer to that question. We can begin now, however, by noting one very basic implication, and some of its practical corollaries.

At its most basic level, the doctrine of the incarnation means that we are at home in the world. We are at home in the world precisely because God is. We belong to the world. Its ways are our ways.

Therefore, we know the physical world in the same way that others know the world. The fallible, self-correcting process of scientific inquiry is not alien to us. We do not have or need a separate, special way of knowing facts about the created order.

Therefore, we participate in the world of values in the same way that others do. The arts and philosophies of our many cultures are all places where God is present. All are vehicles for the expression of the divine, however partially. We do not claim or want to claim some special status for our cultural patterns and modes of thought.

Therefore, we seek the healing of the world alongside of others, working in the same ways that others work. The worldly processes in which justice struggles to be born and grow are the processes in which God is working to bring about wholeness and healing. We do not know of a process of salvation that excludes the psychological, social, political, economic, and cultural dimensions of life.

Therefore, too, our religious yearnings and insights are of a piece with those of others. The incarnation of God means that all of the world's religions are frail but fecund sites of the divine. Seeing God in Christ has taught us that. We may say with John's gospel that no one comes to God except through Christ, but "Christ" is the Christian name for the logos of God in all of creation, including all religions. We do not have a privileged religious perspective, and we do not need one in order to embrace and proclaim our faith.

But just as we hope to learn from other religious traditions, and do, we believe that the incarnation in Jesus, proclaimed in the New Testament, has something of saving value for others to consider and to appropriate according to the light of the divine in their lives.

In the birth of Jesus we see the gentleness and vulnerability of the divine. We believe that God works through ordinariness, not shock and awe, and that caring for the divine work of redemption is everywhere placed in our small human hands.

In the actions of Jesus we see the primacy of God's commitment to the neglected ones. We believe that advocating for the excluded—because of race, class, gender, sexual orientation, and whatever other forms of exclusion become apparent to us—is a continuation of the ministry of Jesus.

In the compassion of Jesus for the least ones we become aware of God's love for all of the creation. We believe we are called to respect and care for the entire creation—human and non-human, spiritual and physical—as the creation loved by God.

In the parables and other teachings of Jesus, we hear God's challenge to every human convention, every status quo. We believe that God calls us to a world that is always more than we have, more than we ask for, more even than we can imagine.

In the persecution of Jesus we witness the seemingly intractable evil that the divine work of salvation everywhere faces. We believe that the redemptive process is a work, a struggle, the success of which is never automatic, its preservation never guaranteed.

In the crucifixion of Jesus we see the willingness of God to suffer and to die, with and for us, if that is what oneness with the world requires. We believe that God's commitment to the world is without limits because it is motivated by unlimited love.

In the resurrection of Jesus we experience the tenacity of a God who will not let go of us or the rest of creation. We believe that no defeat diminishes the divine resolve to seek the human good and the good of the entire created order.

In Jesus Christ we believe we see intimations of a God who is incarnate—a God who is with us fully, and fully, too, with all creation.

POINTS FOR REFLECTION

- The New Testament is an interpretation of Jesus of Nazareth by those whose lives he had transformed. Their interpretations varied because Jesus was experienced differently by different followers.

- The diversity of interpretations of Jesus is not a problem. It is a reservoir to enrich, provoke, and challenge our own interpretations of Jesus. We should maintain this reservoir of manifold understandings.

- Each of the varied interpretations of Jesus calls us to be no less specific today about the meaning of Jesus for our time. For this, quite surprisingly, we might find guidance in the creeds of the ancient councils.

- The claim of Nicea, however arcane it sounds, was extraordinary—it said that the God made present in Jesus is the "truly true" God, not some lesser form of divinity.

- The claim of Constantinople was as audacious as that of Nicea. It insisted that the true God was at one with true humanity, not some unusual or extraordinary humanity.

- The councils at Ephesus and Chalcedon were no less bold. They said the oneness of true divinity and true humanity was not partial; it was full and complete. This is the doctrine of divine "incarnation."

- The councils insisted on the full union of full divinity with full humanity in order to claim that in Jesus full salvation is possible. Underlying their claim was the insight that God saves by becoming one with that which God seeks to save.

- St. Paul claims that salvation is not only for "we ourselves," but also for the "entire created order" (Romans 8). If God becomes one with what God seeks to save, then God is incarnate in the entire creation—fully God, fully world, fully one.

- In Jesus Christ we believe we see intimations of a God who is incarnate—a God who is with us fully, and fully, too, with all creation.

Chapter 4

God:
Exploring the Depths

Americans overwhelmingly believe in God. It is not clear that they overwhelmingly *think* about that belief—what it means, whether it is credible, and its consequences for everyday life. For Christians, however, an unreflective faith is not possible if we take seriously the injunction to love God with the mind as well as the heart and soul. A faith immune to open and self-critical reflection—reflection subject to the full range of evidence at hand—is not a progressive Christian faith. Indeed, it is not an authentic standpoint for any Christian who acknowledges the biblical insistence that we should "be prepared to give a reason for the faith" that guides our lives. It is not clear, however, that we are prepared!

Perhaps it is becoming less easy to believe in God unreflectively. If so, the credit should go in part to the writings of the so-called "militant atheists" whose books currently are bestsellers and the subject of media discussion almost everywhere. Their criticisms are in important ways uninformed about the nature of religion and, in particular, about the history of Christianity.

Even so, their critiques do apply, with a vengeance, to the view of God as all-knowing and all-powerful ruler and judge that characterizes much of American Christianity today. But the militant atheists also criticize more progressive forms of Christian thought. In particular they allege that our progressive perspectives serve only to veil, not replace, the repressive view of deity which, they say, is the true Christian view.

Progressive Christians should listen to the claims of all their adversaries, including these. Not only do they deserve our respect as generally thoughtful seekers of truth, they provide important checks on our temptation as self-described "progressive" thinkers to be too confident of our conclusions. But they are also helpful, if unwitting, allies in the progressive Christian's effort to unmask and reject the repressive view of God that has infected so much of Christianity.

Reclaiming the Incarnate God

Many Christians view God as the all-powerful ruler of the universe whose will controls the direction of human life, the development of history, and the destiny of the entire creation. God is the cosmic monarch. Whatever happens, good or evil, is caused or permitted by this God in "his" infinite wisdom.

There may be temporary comfort in believing that everything is determined or at least permitted by God, but there is also puzzlement and moral distress. One puzzle is why, if all that happens is in accord with the will of God, we should try as diligently as we do to make things better. Why seek to improve upon the course of events that accord with the will of God? Or, if God has ordained that we should seek improvement on the things that "he" has caused or permitted, why did God cause or permit them in the first place? If that is not an intolerably callous way to run a universe, it is, at the least, poor planning.

This intellectual puzzle, however, leads to great personal anguish when it is coupled with the belief that this all-powerful monarch is good and loving. Why, indeed, would a loving God bring about, or even allow, the wasteful destruction that besets nature, history, and every human life? We have human bodies which, although marvelous, could still do with a few design improvements, some of which we have made already. Surely an omnipotent, loving God would do better. We witness human brutality to other humans and to the rest of creation that we, with only limited goodness, know to be outrageous and seek feverishly to end. Surely an omnipotent God could, and if loving would, end or at least diminish the wanton brutality all around us.

In *The Brothers Karamazov*, Ivan challenges his brother Alyosha's belief in the cosmic monarch God.[8] He tells the young monk that he will discount all of the other reasons for rejecting this God and offer only one reason, the suffering of innocent children. Then Ivan recounts the stories he has heard about the cruel mistreatment, neglect, torture, and brutal killing of children, stories like those we read everyday in our newspapers. And then Ivan asks Alyosha one question: If you were God and, in order to bring about this glorious creation, you knew in advance that doing so could result in the suffering of only one innocent child—only one, to say nothing of the millions and millions of children who would suffer—would you, Alyosha, create the world, under those conditions? Alyosha, the pious young monk, is silent, and then he replies. "No, I would not."

The development of belief in a monarchical God is understandable. It emerged in the ancient world when powerful rulers rose up to unify peoples, create laws, impose order, and (ostensibly) protect their subjects from outside threats, natural and human. For a variety of reasons, both humane and lamentable, these developments were deemed to be good. Hence the cause of these developments—the power of the monarch—came to be viewed as the *source* of these goods and thus itself the epitome of what is good. The greater the power, it would have seemed, the greater the good, and, if so, then absolute power would equate to absolute good. Of course, in time it became apparent that no human ruler is absolutely good, and thus none is entitled to absolute power. Even so, the equation of absolute goodness and absolute power could still be made, if now it were ascribed to a divine ruler. The equation was made—God is absolutely good, and so absolutely powerful.

Many traditional Christians, however, have wrestled in the depths of their souls with the question that arises from this view of God. "Why, if God is all-powerful and good, is there so much utterly pointless evil in the world—evil that no outcome could possibly justify, and evil, in fact, that we mortals try desperately to prevent?"

The most credible reply of these anguished Christians is a commendably honest one: "We don't have an answer. We do not understand anymore than did Ivan, Alyosha, or the most rigorous denier of an omnipotent deity. We do not know."

But there is another understanding of God. It is different from the view of God as cosmic monarch. This alternative understanding also emerged in the ancient world. It did not fit well, however, with the growth of empires, nor did it serve the needs of rulers for adulation. It persisted nevertheless, usually in the quiet corners of peasant piety but sometimes, unrecognized, in the councils of ecclesiastical and political power.

It is the view of God as incarnate.

The origin of this view of divinity lies in the Hebrew background of Jesus, his Jewish context, the life he lived, and what this seemed to his followers to imply about the nature of the world and all life—each life, each form of life—within it. This interpretation is a "faith" precisely in the sense that the facts of Jesus' life, whatever they were, and the realities of the world, whatever we discover them to be, are assumed to permit this interpretation, even if they do not require it. It cannot be proven; it can only be proffered and tested continuously against everyday realities—personal, social, natural, and cosmic—for its adequacy as a guide to living in the world.

The fulcrum of this faith is belief in a God who is fully in and with the world. The world is God's place, its processes are the means through which God works, its destiny and that of the divine are intertwined. The chief symbols of this understanding of God are a peasant newborn in a manger, a child growing in knowledge, a teacher of compassion for all things, a prophet opposing injustice, a preacher of new ways of being, and a lonely man hanging on a cross, forgiving his enemies and doubting his faith, who somehow gives rise to a confidence—expressed in different, even conflicting, ways by his followers—that evil is not ultimately victorious.

A manger, a prophet, a cross—these are not the symbols of a cosmic monarch. If they can faithfully symbolize God at all, it will be a God whose place is in the cosmos, with the creation, among the creatures. It will be a God whose reality incorporates the realities of all created life—chance and order, animate and inanimate, human and non-human, living and dying, good and bad, joy and sorrow. It will be a God whose way of creating is the persuasive power of what is best or better for each given situation, large and small. It will be a God whose way of saving is as a presence throughout the creation, as creative energy, judging goodness, healing love.

It will not be a God who makes worlds on command, determines evolution in advance, stops bullets in their flight, topples tyrants from their thrones, or works other magical interventions. It will be a patiently working God. One who inspires the new, undergirds the good, and heals the broken by being fully present in and with the whole creation.

It will be the God made known to us in Jesus Christ.

Thinking about the Incarnate God

There is no one way to think about the incarnate God. John's gospel does so by employing a philosophical idea drawn from the Hellenistic tradition, while the ancient Christian councils used the substance philosophy of the Greeks. We can learn from both, but neither approach, so foreign to our modern way of seeing things, is adequate for us.

Ways of thinking about God appropriate to our time are needed and, fortunately, have begun to appear. Two in particular deserve our attention—Openness Theology (sometimes called Freewill Theism) and a family of views known as Process Theology. Openness Theology began primarily as a re-reading of the Bible but has proceeded to take on, with more intentionality, a supportive philosophical framework. Process Theology developed from a broad philosophical perspective but has continued to evolve and become more diverse as its Christian proponents have revised and expanded it in light of the biblical tradition. Their important differences, largely philosophical in character, need not concern us here. But we should add that these differences are likely to make Openness Theology more congenial to progressive Christians with an evangelical background, and Process Theology more congenial to those whose heritage is liberalism. Our interest is in what the two theologies hold in common. (For readers who wish to explore these views further, John Cobb is perhaps the best known Process theologian, and Clark Pinnock is the leading Openness theologian.[9])

Despite their differences, Process and Openness modes of thought can be summarized together because, in their explicitly Christian theological forms, both begin with the conviction that love is the fundamental character of God. Everything else that is said about God must be compatible with saying that God is love. This means that God is intimately connected to the world, caring for it, and committed to its good. It also means that God, as love, is necessarily sensitive to the world and vulnerable to its developments. As the being of each lover is partly determined by the being of the other, so the being of God and that of the world are intertwined and mutually interactive. God makes a real difference in the world; the world makes a real difference in God.

For our purposes, the key element of love to be considered is the vulnerability that it entails. God is vulnerable; the life of God is a dynamic process that is affected by the world. The joys in our personal lives are joys that make a difference to God. More equitable social and political forms of human community increase the quality of God's life. The advance of ecological justice is an advance in the divine experience.

Vulnerability also means that loss in the world impoverishes God. God suffers in our suffering. God is torn by the persistent injustice of our societies. God is diminished by the mistreatment of the non-human world. God "dies" in the "crucifixions" that we suffer and that we impose on other people and other members of the creation. It may help us to think of the creation in its entirety as the "body" of God. To harm the well-being of that body is to harm the vulnerable God. To advance the well-being of the creation, at any point and in any way, enriches the God who is with us and with the whole creation.

The vulnerability of a loving God leads us rapidly away from the concept of a cosmic monarch and away from many of the familiar ideas that have been associated with it. A God who is open to the world—whether by primordial choice (the Openness position), or metaphysical necessity (the Process position)—cannot do anything that God might wish to do, and cannot know everything that God might desire to know. In other words, at least as we ordinarily think of these terms, God is not "omnipotent" (all-powerful) or "omniscient" (all-knowing).

These ideas may sound radical, even "heretical." After all, for centuries the dominant Christian tradition, addicted to the doctrine of a cosmic monarch, suppressed them. But they seem inescapable if we are to take seriously the biblical vision of a loving God, interactive with the world and affected by it. That, at least, is the judgment of the progressive Christian. The reasons are clear.

The processes of the world in which God is incarnate are characterized by an element of contingency or chance. Further, it is a world in which humans are in some measure free agents, actors who make choices that are not entirely determined by antecedent factors. Openness theologians say that in choosing to bring this kind of world into being, God willingly relinquished the power to abrogate that freedom and, in so doing, accepted willingly the risks of working with and within such a world. Process theologians begin with a different set of assumptions, but the end point is similar: human free choices (and, for them, the processes of nature, too) are inviolate, limiting conditions within which God must work, and, in love, does work willingly. God is not "omnipotent."

The free agency of humans and the contingency or chance throughout the cosmic process means that, at any given point in time, the future is to some degree open, unclear, undecided, indeterminate. To the degree that this is so, the future is also unknown to God. God fully knows the past and present, according to these theologians, and God knows future possibilities as they unfold, but which of these options are to be realized is unsettled for the world and, therefore, also for God. Except as a set of still open possibilities, God does not know the future. In this sense, God is not "omniscient."

God's power in the world is conceived somewhat differently by Openness and Process theologians (as well as differently within the Process movement itself). Openness theologians speak of God's power primarily as inspiration, usually in conjunction with reference to the Holy Spirit. Process theologians use that language, too, but they also speak of the "persuasive power of ideal forms of becoming" as the means through which God makes a difference in human experience and other natural processes. In more naturalistic versions of Process Theology, the divine agency is conceived not as a person, but as a cosmic principle or process (such as "creativity," or as a "power that makes for right")—one element of the universe among others.

In all of these progressive concepts of God, however, the autonomy of human beings (and for Process Theologies, the independence of non-human processes, too) are not, and cannot be, abrogated by God. Thus the course of things moves forward—in the cosmos, nature, history, and individual human life—through the interaction of multiple, interdependent causes at many different levels, including the persuasive agency of the relational God of love. At every point at every level, God is active through the inspiration of the best possibilities for that impasse, everywhere in the universe.

The incarnate God *is* omnipresent!

Experiencing the Incarnate God

Christian faith in God, like every other vital religious faith, is experiential as well as conceptual. It is a combination, in action, of the rational and the passionate, of ideas and feelings. Although, as we've seen, progressive Christians think of God in ways that differ markedly from the monarchical tradition, the various ways in which they experience God are like those of Christians throughout the ages. For example, the incarnate God is experienced as guide, as presence, and as mystery.

The most common way that Christians talk about God and God's impact in their lives is as divine guide. The incarnate God is a "right-seeking" God. God's role in the universe is to nudge it from less to more adequate forms and processes (which are not necessarily more complex or orderly in character). So for humans, God is the "lure" or push toward more wholesome forms of being within the self, within our societies, with the rest of the creation, and therefore also with God. The call to repent and move away from self-centeredness, beyond racism, sexism, and homophobia, and toward economic and ecological justice is an experience of God.

God is also experienced as a presence, an immediacy that is intrinsically valuable, valuable simply for its being-with-us. A gripping experience of nature—a sunset over the mountains, a view of earth from outer space, frost on fallen autumn leaves—is not "merely" an experience of nature; it is also an experience of the God incarnate in nature. An experience of communion with another individual or within a community of individuals is a good in itself. It needs no outcome beyond itself in order to be a benefit. It is also an experience of the God incarnate in human relationships. A sense that God, the ultimate good, is not elsewhere, is not here on occasion, but is here in the world fully and pervasively, is an experience of the presence of God incarnate.

God is experienced as mystery. The idea of a God who is fully one with the creation does not diminish the divine mystery, but underscores it. The mystery of God incarnate does not depend on the mystifying language and concepts of the christological councils. It appears already in the very notion that there is a directional power at work in what, by most accounts, seems to be a purely contingent, even whimsical, cosmic process. It is more than readily evident in the confidence that amidst the vicissitudes of history, the interminable struggles of social life, and the frustrating perplexities of individually trying to know and do the good, there is at work—precisely in these mundane and ambiguous processes—a power that offers to us and the entire creation the forms of healing for which we long, toward which we strive, but which we can articulate in only the barest, most tentative terms.

The preservation of an appropriate sense of mystery may be the greatest gift that belief in God has to offer our world today. It does not hamper the quest for truth, it tempers that quest with modesty. It does not enervate the search for justice, it tempers it with humility. It does not weaken our capacity to hope, it fills us with patient expectation.

Faith in the Incarnate God

A religion is a comprehensive orientation toward life. It is the framework within which we understand ourselves, our meaning and place in our larger environments, and how we should live within them. In other words, a religion is a way of life. Ideas of God are the fundamental interpretive point of view that grounds this orientation and holds it together. God is the key, so to speak, for understanding what the framework implies about our meaning, the meaning of our world, and our proper role in it. How we, as Christians, think we ought to live is grounded in our concept of God.

Our concept of God, however, is always an interpretation, never a straightforward description of what is there for all to see. We certainly believe it to be a plausible interpretation of the world, and in our daily lives, if we are reflective Christians, we test the adequacy of our understanding of God. But it is never provable. For this reason, our view of God, though fundamental, is *never, ever* a legitimate source of absolute claims or absolute attitudes.

The "absolutizing" of religion and religious belief is a sign of fear, a desperate attempt to hide the fact that our fundamental orientations toward life are always interpretive adventures, always a risk. Critics of religion are fully justified in denouncing its absolutistic expressions. They misunderstand religion, though, when they assume that the absolutistic impulse is essential to it. On the contrary, it is a corruption of religion precisely because religion is a standpoint of faith. All too often, however, Christians, still under the spell of a monarchical deity, illustrate that corruption vividly, and destructively. Christian faith, which ought to banish fear, becomes its mask.

POINTS FOR REFLECTION

- Many Christians view God as the cosmic monarch whose will controls all things. There may be temporary comfort in this view of God, but there is also puzzlement and great moral distress.

- Belief in a monarchical God emerged in the ancient world when powerful rulers rose up to unify people, impose order, and provide protection.

- There is another understanding of God. It did not fit well with the growth of empires, but it persisted nevertheless. It is the view of God as incarnate.

- A manger, a prophet, a cross—these are not the symbols of a cosmic monarch. They symbolize a patiently working God, one who inspires, undergirds, and heals by being present. This is the incarnate God made known to us in Jesus Christ.

- Progressive Christian understandings of God begin with the conviction that love is God's fundamental character. Love is vulnerable, and the vulnerability of God leads us rapidly away from the concept of a cosmic monarch.

- The incarnate God is experienced as guide, presence, and mystery—as the call to move toward more wholesome ways of being, as the immediacy felt in communion with others, as the sustaining confidence in a power that works for good in all things.

- Awareness of God's mystery does not hamper the quest for truth; it tempers that quest with modesty. It does not enervate the search for justice, it tempers it with humility. It does not weaken our capacity to hope, it fills us with patient expectation.

- The "absolutizing" of our religious beliefs is a sign of fear, and a corruption of faith. All too often, Christians, under the spell of a monarchical deity, illustrate that corruption vividly and destructively. Christian faith, which ought to banish fear, becomes its mask.

Chapter 5

Humanity:
Continuing the Creation

Three questions are fundamental to our experience as humans: Who are we to be? How should we live? and, Why do we fail to be and live as we should? We may not often ask these questions aloud, but we do not need to because we "feel" them daily. They are at the base of our everyday quandaries as ordinary folk and at the base of the philosophical outlooks that undergird our cultures. Not surprisingly, then, they are also fundamental theological questions.

If people are to consider Christianity seriously as a way of life, they are likely to do so initially because they think Christianity addresses these three questions in insightful and transformative ways. Indeed, more often than not what Christians say about Jesus, God, salvation, and the Church begins to get a hearing among others because of what Christianity has to say about being human. And the truth is that the strongest believer may from time to time question various aspects of Christian teaching—and those questions are to be valued—but what binds her or him into this tradition is its understanding of being human. Christians, like other people, begin with the human questions because we are human.

Who are We to Be?

For Christianity, who we are to be as human beings and what we are to do are inextricably connected. It would be wrong to claim that there is a single Christian viewpoint on these issues, but there certainly is a "family" of related viewpoints with common themes. As one might expect, the themes are most effectively communicated in the myths, stories, and symbols repeated throughout the biblical tradition and the history of the Church. Our reflective beliefs as Christians grow out of these "story" traditions as they bear upon and illuminate daily experience. So, too, our views of being human. These are not philosophical in nature, though they have implications for more abstract conceptions of being human. They are practical. And they focus in particular on the distinctive kind of responsibility that humans are given, and the special type of norms that should guide our exercise of that responsibility.

An especially interesting "introduction" to a Christian view of being human is a story found in the long set of creation myths and legends in the Book of Genesis. This story is found in Genesis 2. It is brief, and explosive in its implications. In this, the second account of creation offered in Genesis (beginning 2:4b), God creates *adam,* which here means "humanity," along with the rest of the creation, not at the end of the creative process. But then, in verses 19–20, God does something quite remarkable. God brings before *adam* the entire array of living things that God has created and tells him to name them: "And whatever the man called every living creature, that was its name."

A name in the Hebraic tradition is not a label for something. It is a designation of that thing's meaning and place. To name something is to decide where it belongs, how it relates to the rest of the creation. In the Genesis 2 story, God brings things into being, and gives to *adam* responsibility for deciding how best to order them. God creates this world; humanity is to arrange it. So much for the view that the world is presented to us readymade! On the contrary, humanity is responsible— that is, response-able—for continuing the creative process, seeking the best ways to order and relate the things that have been made.

Creative responsibility—or, perhaps, responsible creativity!— is the theme of this story. It is a theme central to the entire biblical tradition. And the very fact that, in this story, God gives to *adam* the task of deciding, must mean that there are real decisions, real options, multiple ways that life might fruitfully be ordered. If there were not, there would be no point in telling *adam* to decide. No doubt there are also multiple ways that things should not be ordered—we must get to that, too. Further, there is the more troublesome fact that we don't pursue the forms of order that we know we should—that is a discussion for the next chapter on sin. The basic point here is about "creative responsibility" as the defining mark of being human. We are not called to conform to an already established plan; we are the creatures who are called to name the things God has created. Or, as the rabbis taught, our task is to assist in continuing the creation, as co-creators with God.

This is a more subtle version of the claim that appears also in the first creation story (Genesis 1:1–2:4a), namely that humans are given "dominion" over the earth. The common interpretation of human dominion has had disastrous consequences.

It has been an excuse, especially since the industrial revolution, for virtually any use of the rest of the creation that might increase human delight, advance human comfort, and multiply human wealth. It has led, using a metaphor introduced in the last chapter, to the rape of the "body of God."

The idea of "human dominion" asserted in Genesis and throughout the biblical tradition, however, is a far cry from any license to exploit the rest of creation. First, it is not an entitlement or privilege granted to humans; it is a job, a work assignment. Second, it is a task to which we are called within a set of givens; the basic ingredients of creation are already established. Finally, it is a task given to humans who are fully a part of the web of creation, not to special beings who are above it. The pervasive tone of the Genesis stories is a sense of the massive interconnectedness of things. Naming the animals, exercising dominion, is a task we are to undertake for the good of the whole, of which we are but one valuable part.

The same understanding of dominion is even more pointedly expressed in the New Testament's paradigmatic idea of "dominion," namely, the "lordship" of Jesus Christ. Christ the Lord, in the New Testament, is the Christ who comes to serve, explicitly rejecting anything like the role of kings who "lord it over their subjects" (Mark 10:42). If we continue to harbor any illusions about what human "dominion" means, it should now be clear: in the biblical tradition and, certainly, from a Christian standpoint, *lordship is servanthood.*

Being given dominion means being responsible for serving the needs of the whole creation, of which we are a part. It is not a place of privilege over the rest of creation to which we are called; it is to a role of special responsibility within the creation. That is central to the meaning of being human.

What are We to Do?

Clearly there are limits to our ability to name the animals. We cannot choose to "re-name" the so-called laws of nature. More important, even among the real alternatives, some possible forms of order should be avoided. But how are we to know? What are the guides?

Following the Jewish tradition, Jesus named two guides, the two "great commandments." First, we are to love God with all our heart, mind, and strength. Second, which is "like unto the first," we are to love our neighbor as ourself. Those are our guides in deciding how to care for God's creation.

It is interesting that the interconnectedness which characterizes creation, according to Genesis, appears again in these commandments. We are to love God with all the parts of our being, not just some. Further, our love of God is connected to our love of neighbor—the latter obligation "is like" the former. Finally, love of neighbor is connected to love of self. Our love of God, which connects our whole being, is a love connected to our love of neighbor, which in turn is connected to our love of self. The love that is to guide our naming is a connected love, holding together and balancing the lover and the loved.

Two points deserve special emphasis. First, serving the other is based on a healthy love, one that includes, rather than excludes, the love of the self. "Love your neighbor as [you love] yourself." Servanthood may involve self-giving, but it is not self-diminishing. It is the freely chosen self-giving of a self that loves itself. Self-giving does not grow out of a hatred or abject denial of the self, its worth, and its needs. Rather, it grows out of personal, social, and spiritual strength, the giving of which will contribute to the health of the whole of which one is a part.

And, we might add, to whom greater strength is given, greater self-giving may be required. Self-giving and self-love are held in balance.

Second, love of God and love of neighbor are inseparable. But how? How can love of God in any way be "like" love of neighbor? The answer is that the neighbor is one in whom the self-giving God is incarnate! Love of God requires love of the neighbor because God is incarnate in the neighbor.

The next step in seeking to understand what we are to do is to ask, "Who is my neighbor?" The answer is expressed in those shocking sayings of Matthew 25: "Just as you have done it to one of the least of these," Jesus says, "you did it to me." It appears, too, in the story of the Good Samaritan. The point of the parable is simple and radical: the neighbor is whoever is in need. Whoever! This radical statement of our obligation overturns our common practices of service, practices that extend readily to family, friends, and others who think and live as we do. These more comfortable "lines of obligation" are superseded by the claim that our obligation is to all, but proportionate to their need, and so especially to the "least of these."

This notion of our obligation is radical because it is at once so personal and so comprehensive, so immediate and so cosmic. It extends to the neighbor-in-need and neighbors-in-need, to the stranger-in-need and to populations of strangers-in-need, to the other . . . to the alien . . . and to the enemy. . . . It extends, too, to the earth.

Our obligation to serve the well-being of the earth is a straightforward consequence of belief in the incarnation. From John's gospel on, Christians have believed that God is incarnate in what God seeks to save. And the claim of

Romans 8 is that God seeks the salvation of the "entire created order." God is in all things, seeking to bring healing and wholeness to all things, to the whole creation, to the entire community of the cosmos. Those who seek to serve this God seek to serve what God serves.

If the interdependence of the world were not obvious enough already, it would in any case follow from Christian belief in the incarnation of God in all things. The creation is literally a "uni-verse"—that which has been turned into one. Each part has value, in the Christian view of things. In Genesis, each segment of creation is judged by God to be of intrinsic worth. In the gospels, each small creature is an object of God's tender care. But each part also has worth for the rest of creation. "Disease" in any part of the creation diminishes the health of the whole. Put in the terms of Paul's audacious vision, God cannot seek to save any part without seeking the salvation of the whole. Nor can we. That is why our obligation is first of all to "the least of these," those human and non-human places in the creation where need is greatest.

Guidance for Naming

Christianity provides a clear understanding of the human role in creation. It does not offer rules for exercising that responsibility. Any attempt to establish abiding rules is a mistake. They are not provided in the Bible or in the teachings of the Church. They are not provided in the teachings of Jesus, either, if we take seriously the New Testament understandings of Jesus. Our abiding guide is the two great commandments, love God and love thy neighbor. Jesus said the degree to which all legal and prophetic traditions are valid for us depends on—"hangs on" (Matthew 22:37)—the extent to which they fulfill these two commandments in their specific contexts.

These two commandments represent the abiding obligation of the progressive Christian. The specific social and ethical decisions of times gone by, like our own moral judgments, are fallible, culturally limited attempts to give expression to these two commandments. We have much to learn from past applications, their weaknesses as well as their strengths, and we must be willing to hear the criticisms of our fallible judgments implicit in their judgments. But to let past "namings" replace our judgments is to shirk *our* responsibility to name the animals in our time and place.

In chapter 2 we saw that the authority of the Bible does not lie in its stipulation of one particular set of beliefs and practices to which we must conform. It cannot be that kind of authority if we are honest about the Bible—if, that is, we acknowledge the irreducibly diverse ways of thinking and acting conveyed in the Scriptures. What the Bible does communicate to us is a process of "pious" (in the best sense) witness, critique, response, and failure and growth. It is a process into which we are invited. We are taught through our participation in that deeply pious process. It authors us, forms us, feeds us, even when we depart from the judgments it conveys that were made for other times and places.

On important theological and practical matters, the Bible embraces difference. Partly for this very reason, Christians today differ in theology, modes of life, and decisions about human relationships. Acceptance of diversity, however, does not mean indifferent relativism. If there are not perfect ways to love God and the neighbor, in each circumstance some ways are far better than others. But diversity remains, and it should.

Continuing diversity in the Church and in the human community seems to be the means by which the incarnate God restrains our longing for absolute perspectives and the arrogance they always engender. Differences provoke us to seek the better ways and prod us to do so in humility.

Another story from Genesis makes this point—the story of the tower of Babel in Genesis 11. Once upon a time, the story goes, people spoke one language and used words in the same way—they were in agreement on things. This unanimity prompted in them the illusion that they were absolutely right and thus they deserved to ascend into the heavens, sharing the place of God. God saw the human arrogance that uniformity gives rise to, so decided to force humans into diversity by giving them different languages. With different languages come different ways of life, different thought-forms, different religions and cultures.

Probably this is an ancient story that the Hebrews shared with other people of the time, a story intended to explain the diversity of human languages. But the story is theologically profound. It does not say that God separated people into different linguistic groups as a punishment—not at all. The diversity imposed on the human race was a safeguard, a protection against the illusion that we are or can become like God. God intervened when uniformity became excessive.

Diversity is essential to a healthy church and a healthy human community. It is God-given, according to Genesis. Not as punishment, but as a check on the presumption of perfection in every human community, religious or cultural, and as a means whereby each human community critiques and enriches the others.

We do not need to take these stories literally in order to see that they say something of importance about God and the ways of the world. Difference is a part of God's creative plan for the world. And if, as progressive Christians believe, God is present throughout the creation, then we must honor each form of life, each culture, each religion, with the understanding that each is a way that humans have exercised their obligation to order life, it is their way of "naming" their worlds.

This very diversity, however, reminds us that no one viewpoint, no way of life, no culture, no religion is perfect. Each is a human undertaking. God's gracious presence in human life everywhere is always refracted through fallible, human beings. For this reason, we must not only honor each tradition, we must also look at it critically. Indeed, we only truly honor a tradition if we care enough about it to seek to identify its failings, and encourage its self-criticism and change.

To honor a tradition is to approach it as a place that in some manner holds the imprint of God's grace and power. To criticize a point of view, which is part of honoring it, is to ask where it is lacking the fullness of God's grace, as understood from our perspective, and how it might become more wholesome and healing. As critics of other traditions, we are not without failings ourselves. So our critical observations and suggestions are themselves fallible. Just as we "honor through examination" other forms of Christianity, other religions, other social and cultural practices, so we expect ourselves to be critiqued, challenged and, possibly, changed by them. An authentic diversity is an engaged diversity; it is one in which our differences with each other are expressed, confronted, and reflected on with resolve.

Of course, an engaged diversity is frustrating, sometimes to the point of despair. The reason is clear. In most cases, our differences are about matters of great importance, about whether in fact we are loving God and neighbor in the best way. We differ in our judgments about what loving means. Many of our current controversies—about homosexuality and same-sex marriage, abortion and stem-cell research, taxation and economic policy, racism and affirmative action, freedom and national security, the environment and eco-justice, immigration and citizenship—are differences of this sort. These differences distress us because the issues are so important. However difficult, we must continue to struggle with them together.

But seeking to know the good, however vital, is not the most important question we face. According to the wisdom of the Christian tradition there is another problem of even greater moment. It is not doing the good that we do know!

Christianity calls this "sin." It is the topic of the next chapter.

POINTS FOR REFLECTION

- More often than not, what Christians have to say about Jesus, God, salvation, and the church get a hearing among others because of what Christianity has to say about being human.

- According to Genesis 2, God creates the world but humans are to arrange it, to order it. We are not called to conform to an already established plan. Our task is to assist in continuing the creation, as co-creators with God.

- Genesis says humans are given "dominion" over the earth. Dominion is not a special entitlement or privilege; it is a vocation of service undertaken for the good of the whole creation.

- What are our guides in deciding how to care for the creation? Jesus named two interconnected guides—to love God, and to love others as we love ourselves.

- Who is the neighbor? The neighbor, understood biblically, is the one or ones in need—individuals and groups, friends and strangers, allies and enemies, and the earth itself.

- Christianity does not offer rules applicable for all times. Our abiding guide is the two great commandments. The validity of other teachings depends on the extent to which they fulfill these commandments in specific contexts.

- Diversity is essential to a healthy church and a healthy human community. It is a God-given check on the presumption of perfection in every human community, a means whereby we critique and enrich each other.

- No one way of life, culture, or religion is perfect. God's gracious presence everywhere is refracted through fallible human beings. For this reason we must not only honor each tradition, we must also look at it critically.

Chapter 6
Sin:
Failing and Hiding

The Christian "doctrine" of sin is not a morbid prescription for guilt or a tirade on the topic of human worthlessness. Or at least it should not be. Discussions of sin should help us see what is going on about us and within us as well. The aim should be to give us insight into our personal and collective failings, not just the simple ones but also the complex failings that seem to continue despite our best intentions. And, in fact, a profound understanding of sin might enable us to see failings that we had not previously noticed, even if at some level we had felt them.

Finally, an analysis of sin should provide us with greater insight into the dynamics of our failings—why and how they happen—and bring us to the question, to be addressed in the next chapter, about how healing is possible. Talk about sin should be a means whereby we see ourselves more clearly, act more humanely, and learn to work more effectively for a better future for ourselves and our planet.

That said, we must acknowledge that discussions of sin, in American Christianity especially, have not been very useful. This is due in part to the way that, historically, sin-talk has seemed—and, in fact, has been—anti-world, anti-sex, anti-female, anti-pleasure, anti-pride, anti-hope, and opposed to equality and self-affirmation, just to mention a few of its drawbacks! To circumvent these consequences, the notion of sin has over time been "revised." In most cases, however, the revision has been pretty shallow—sin is a lag in human evolution (what can we do about that?), a quaint name for psychological maladies (why add to the mystification of psychological lingo?), a deviation from majority expectations (that's bad?), or a violation of somebody else's favorite Bible verses, which is especially shallow because everybody can win that game.

If it is to be worthy of a hearing, progressive Christianity must articulate an insightful and constructive understanding of sin, one that makes a difference to human understanding and potentially to human behavior. And to do so, I think progressive Christians would be well-advised to look again at the historic resources of Christian tradition. However difficult it might be to unhook those resources from the abuses of the past and the misunderstandings to which they have given rise, the effort just might pay off. It's true that much in historic Christian talk about sin has been sick and oppressive. But underneath the layers of disease and destruction there is, I believe, a great deal of insight to contemplate and appropriate for a Christian vision that will truly be progressive in today's world.

Let me explain.

The Forms of Sin: Pride and Sensuality

In classical theology, sin takes two forms, pride and sensuality. Already our hackles are raised because we are all supportive of pride—in ourselves, our families and children (*and* our grandchildren!), our nation, our human achievements. So the question is obvious: What's wrong with pride? And why should anyone think sensuality is a sin? Of course we may be a bit more self-conscious about saying so, but the sensual, too, is a value that we affirm; sensuality is a part of healthy human experience. Pride and sensuality are good. How can a tradition that labels them "sin" have anything to teach us?

To answer this question, I suggest that we examine what, fundamentally, these terms meant in the Christian tradition. Let's ask, What insights into human behavior and relationships did they supposedly provide? Then we can decide whether or not there is anything of worth in the underlying concepts, even if we may not want to retain the terms themselves.

We can start with St. Paul (who, for some reason, thought a lot about sin). In Romans 12:3, Paul says to the congregation, "I say to everyone among you not to think of yourself more highly than you ought to think." That, basically, is what the theological tradition came later to speak of as "pride." It is excessive self-regard, not adhering to appropriate limits, taking for oneself more than that to which one is entitled. In language more appropriate for today, the sin of pride is too much pride, excessive self-regard.

"Sensuality" referred to the opposite failing—too little pride, inadequate self-regard, limiting oneself too much, expecting for oneself less than that to which one is entitled.

We can imagine why "pride" was used to refer to inordinate self-regard, but why did the tradition use "sensuality" to refer to expecting too little of oneself?

The answer reflects one of the more unseemly aspects of the ancient and medieval (and modern?) Christian traditions. The sensual was associated with the sexual, and both with the "lower" part of human nature, our "animal" side. So being sensual, in this view, was being animal-like, driven by passion. Sensuality referred to the failure to rise up and act responsibly; failing to exercise the freedom and power that is presumably distinctive of being human. In sum, if pride was, in a sense, pretending to be more than an ordinary human, sensuality was pretending to be less.

These, then, are the two basic expressions of sin, according to Christian tradition. Pride is thinking of oneself more highly than one ought to think; sensuality is thinking of oneself less highly than one ought to think.

We can translate this traditional understanding of the forms of sin into a different language, using as our reference point the two great commandments. The love these commandments require, we noted in chapter 5, is an interconnected and balanced love, a love fitting to the object of love. In light of these commandments, then, sin is disproportionate love, love that is out of balance—excessive or deficient love.

Stated abstractly, sin is an affirmation of oneself that neglects the needs of the neighbor, or an affirmation of those like us that fails to show love for those who are different, or a love for humanity that fails to affirm the intrinsic worth of the rest of creation, or a love for the creation that does not also love God. Sin is also the reverse of these: sin is loving God but neglecting the creation in which God is incarnate, or loving the rest of creation but diminishing humanity, or devoting oneself to those who are different with little regard for one's own kind, or devoting oneself to the neighbor and ignoring one's own needs.

In life, of course, excessive or deficient love is not abstract. It is concrete. In its most grotesque forms sin is the things we condemn as criminal—murder, slavery, torture, rape, and abuse. But sin has more subtle forms, too. It is the husband who leaves it up to his wife to handle her job, attend to the house, and care for the kids. It is the woman who passes up the opportunity for an education because she lacks self-esteem. It is the person transfixed by televised trivia while nations are bombed and villages are burned. It is the progressive Christian who works for social justice but neglects the inner life of the spirit. It is the activist who defends minorities for a living and demeans them in private conversation. It is the champion of legal rights for the unborn but not health care for the born. It is the parents who love their own children but ignore the thousands of others who each year are forced into sexual slavery. It is the preacher who says love is the greatest of virtues except when it joins together gays or lesbians. It is the industry that allows its CEO to earn 300 times the median income of its employees. It is the economic system that permits the top 1% of earners to receive 22% of the nation's income, and the top 10% to earn nearly half. It is the society that permits a 25% poverty rate among blacks compared to an 8% rate among whites. It is the educational system that spends three to five times as much on children of the rich as on children of the middle class and poor minorities. It is the nation that looks upon itself as uniquely virtuous and its adversaries as uniquely evil. It is the countries with 12% of the world's population that produce

58% of its carbon emissions. It is the species that oppresses and diminishes the rest of nature for its own convenience and gratification. It is the religion that claims to have a privileged perspective on absolute truth. Sin is the Christian who does not rise up against these instances of grossly, even obscenely, unbalanced love.

Sin, in a progressive Christian view of things, is loving too much or loving too little any part of the interconnected web of life, from God to all of those whom God loves and in whom God is incarnate, including the very least ones.

This understanding of sin or human failing is not widely debated (which is not to say it is widely heeded). Of course we may differ on some details, but in general this view of sin as "pride" and "sensuality" is shared (often using other terms) by Catholics and Protestants and, among the latter, by Wesleyans and Calvinists. Indeed, it may be shared by religions generally. Loving God, self, and the human and non-human neighbor is really a Christian elaboration of the Golden Rule, "Do unto others as you would have them do unto you." And in one form or another, this injunction appears to be an ideal in Christianity, Judaism, Islam, Hinduism, Buddhism, Confucianism, and the traditions of indigenous tribal communities. So at least by implication there is pretty general agreement, too, on what it would mean for humans to fail.

This widely shared understanding of sin casts a searing light on our failings, and it is vitally important. But the analysis of sin, at least in the more insightful traditions of Christian reflection, goes one important step further; it seeks to understand why sin in all its manifestations has such tremendous staying power. Why is our failure to love as we ought so persistent, so pervasive? According to this tradition of Christian reflection, the answer has something to do with self-deception, hiding the truth from ourselves.

The Strategy of Sin—Self-Deception

The idea of deception appears rather often in discussions of sin in the Bible, starting at the beginning when Eve says, "The serpent tricked me, and I ate." It continues into the New Testament and is most fully developed in the writings of Paul. Romans 1, a kind of "theo-psychoanalysis" of sin and deceit, is interesting enough to quote:

> For the wrath of God is revealed from heaven against all ungodliness and wickedness of those who by their wickedness suppress the truth. For what can be known about God is plain to them, because God has shown it to them. . . . So they are without excuse; for although they knew God, they did not honor God or gives thanks to him, but they become futile in their thinking, and their senseless minds were darkened. Claiming to be wise, they became fools. . . . (18–22)

The ingenious strategy of sin, Paul says, is its power of self-deception. Those who sin, he says, not only sin, they also "suppress the truth" about their doing so. Not only do they fail to honor God (here we might substitute "honor the commandments to love"), they also cease to be aware of this fact. Their self-understanding, therefore, cannot be trusted because they have become "futile in their thinking," their minds have become "darkened," unable to sense the truth about their failure to love as they should.

In Paul's view, those who fail to love properly are deceived about that failure, but—and here is the stunning claim—that deception is self-imposed. They are deceived and they have done it to themselves—they are self-deceived! After all, according to Paul, they "knew God." "What can be known about God," he insists, "is plain to them, because God has shown it to them." So they are "without excuse" precisely because, although they no longer know of their failure to honor God, their ignorance is ingeniously self-created and self-imposed. It is for this reason, as Paul says in 1 Corinthians 4, that he cannot count himself "acquitted" even though he is not aware of anything against himself. Only God, he adds, can reliably know "the things now hidden in darkness." Still, those who fail to love properly cannot excuse themselves because, at one level, they know the truth that, at another level, they do not know. How is that possible? They have hidden the truth from themselves.

This is the additional claim about sin that we should consider. Sin is not simply the failure to love properly in all of the ways we have enumerated. It is that failure accompanied by an intricate hiding strategy; it is the failure to love properly and the pretense that we have not failed to love properly. We hide that truth, even from ourselves!

This is a very troubling charge against us. It is not—we should be careful to note—the claim that we never love as we should, and it is not the claim that we always lie to ourselves about our failings. It certainly is not the assertion that "there is no good in us." But it is the claim that we fail and hide a good deal more than we like to admit. Indeed, a great deal more.

If we wish to test this harsh hypothesis, we might set aside Paul's ancient categories ("wrath of God," "wickedness of men," "futile thinking," "darkened minds") and directly test his basic point, about self-deception, against our own experience, beginning with our experience of others. Have we noticed any self-deception recently?

If we have, it might be among a few political leaders who, for example, trumpet economic policies that supposedly benefit all by immediately benefiting those who are the wealthiest, or health insurance policies that supposedly benefit all by initially benefiting the insurers; or international policies that supposedly protect our freedoms by basically protecting international finance. In a cynical mood we might think that they know the truth and baldly lie to us, but it is at least as likely that they have persuaded themselves of what to the rest of us is pretty clearly false. They do not know the truth, even though Paul says somewhere deep within they do know because they have hidden it from themselves.

If we have noticed a bit of self-deception lately, it might be someone among the famous religious leaders who, for example, preach that homosexuality is an abomination (or at least an ungodly disease) but engage in homosexual acts on occasion when they are under stress; or who defend the economic interests of the tenuous middle class but never criticize special tax breaks for clergy; or who use the mass media to raise money for God while they build their mansions and buy their Ferraris. We might think they are lying to us; perhaps they have succeeded in lying to themselves, too.

It is not unheard of that a company executive might squirrel away millions while the employee pension funds diminish and insist it was innocent, or an employer might promote a favored staff member on specious grounds and insist it was proper, or a professional activist on behalf of the poor might regularly fly first class and ride in limousines and insist it is necessary, or a shop owner might . . . or a colleague might . . . or a lover or spouse or parent or sibling or neighbor might. . . . We can fill in the blanks.

Now to the difficult conclusion: *In addition to all of these other people, it is part of St. Paul's understanding of sin that all of us engage in self-deception!*

Was our collusion with patriarchy, whether we are male or female, entirely the result of a twisted cultural inheritance, or did we know, somewhere and to some degree, that this arrangement was just not right? We knew, but hid it from ourselves, according to Paul. And what of our acceptance of racial privilege if we are white, or our accommodation to the economic exploitation of the Third World if we are North Americans, or our blind eye to the plight of the homeless if we are housed, or our silence about homophobia if we are straight, or our impoverishment of nature until nature's suffering threatened our own welfare? Did we not know? If not, who so cleverly hid the truth from us?

Here is the point: According to Paul's harsh hypothesis, we all act, participate in, or acquiescence to, actions that fail miserably to love as love should be shown. And, Paul adds, we carefully, skillfully, convincingly hide these failings from ourselves.

What is the result? The answer is what Christianity has often labeled "original sin."

The Structure of Sin—Original Sin

The Christian doctrine of original sin has a terrible reputation, deservedly so—at least in its popular rendition. It is said to mean that we are sinners from birth, that we are "worms," that there is "no good in us," and, worse, that we get into this awful state because of sex. Well, that's not what the doctrine really means, but I will try to make its point by appealing to a non-biblical source.

"Mine the Harvest" is a poem by Edna St. Vincent Millay, an American poet of the first half of the twentieth century. In it, Millay (disclosure: she was no saint!) speaks about the effort to make the world better. "This should be simple," she writes, "if one's power were great, if one were God, for instance . . . to manipulate and mould unwieldy, heavy, obstinate but thoughtless matter, into some bright world." For nothingness is "plastic," she explains, and in the right hands should be "easy to bend." In the next verse, however, Millay sees the human condition as anything but malleable, for now, she notes, we are not beginning at the start but after a long and sad history, one that cannot easily be peeled away. She writes of the human condition as evil laid down upon evil, layer after layer throughout the centuries, like a thick laminate of sedimentary rock—"layers uncountable as leaves in coal."

The Christian doctrine of original sin is about the "evil upon evil" that "laminate" the structures of our existence. It is about the fact that we do not start from the beginning. It is about the fact that these inherited structures are stubborn givens and take possession of our world and of our individual being—they are both external and internal. They are "givens" out there—racism, sexism, classism, heterosexism, ageism, speciesism, materialism, consumerism, egotism . . . and what else? We are born into these, they are inculcated in us. We begin with them. We have no other starting place.

But it is not as if, apart from that, we are innocent, pure souls who just happened to get placed in some awful environment.

These layers of evil lie within us, too. The structures we inherit are internalized, easily and pleasantly ingested rather like our mother's milk. There is a lovely passage from the *Confessions* of St. Augustine that makes the point: "Thus with the baggage of the world I was sweetly burdened, as one in slumber, and my musings on thee were like the efforts of those who desire to awake, but who are still overpowered with drowsiness and fall back into deep slumber. . . ."[10]

With the evils of the world we are "sweetly burdened." Languishing as in a nap on a warm summer day, our awareness of these realities moves vaguely onto the fringes of consciousness. But, usually, after brief and dreamy glimpses of these evils, we let them go and slip back into our slumbers. And so we continue in our collusion with evil.

That is the view of sin that I think progressive Christians should consider: We fail, we hide, and our failings and hidings build into seemingly binding, but comfortable, modes of life in which love of God and others is manipulated, twisted, cheapened, distorted, denied, or virtually destroyed.

If we think this view of the human condition is at least close to being right, we might be moved to utter a biblical lament that heretofore would probably have seemed a bit overdone, echoing Paul's words to the Romans: "The whole creation has been groaning in labor pains" (8:23). We might even cry in despair, "Oh wretched mess that we're in! Who will rescue us?" At about this point, however, another biblical conviction could conceivably come to mind. It is the strangely confident insistence that there is a Power at work within us, *just as we are*, that is able to do far more than we ask, more, indeed, than we can even imagine.

That's the topic of the next chapter.

POINTS FOR REFLECTION

- Modern discussions of sin have not been very useful. Sin-talk has been anti-world, anti-sex, anti-female, anti-pleasure, and opposed to equality and self-affirmation, just to mention a few of its drawbacks.

- In classical Christian theology, sin takes two forms, pride and sensuality. Already our hackles are raised! We are all supportive of pride, and why should anyone think sensuality is a sin?

- By "pride" the tradition meant excessive self-regard in relation to others, assuming for oneself more than that to which one is entitled. "Sensuality" meant the opposite failure, thinking of oneself less highly than one ought to think.

- Viewed in terms of the two great commandments, sin is loving too much, or loving too little, any part of the interconnected web of life, from God to all of those whom God loves and in whom God is incarnate.

- The more insightful Christian traditions ask, Why is our failure to love as we ought so persistent and pervasive? The answer it gives has to do with self-deception, hiding the truth from ourselves.

- Sin is not simply the failure to love properly. It is that failure accompanied by the pretense that we have loved as we should. We hide our failure, even from ourselves!

- The doctrine of "original sin" is not a denial of human goodness, and it is not about sex. It is about the layers of evil—racism, sexism, consumerism, egotism, etc.—structured into our existence. We begin our lives in the midst of these.

- Christian tradition "suspects" that we rather happily acquiesce to the evil structures in which we find ourselves. Our failings build into unjust and self-serving structures . . . and we find them to be quite comfortable!

Chapter 7
Salvation: Seeking and Finding

American culture is awash in offers of salvation. Usually such offers admit to being limited in scope—the salvation of your back from pain, your nights from sleeplessness, your marriage from boredom, your children from mediocrity, your mind from shallowness, your home from foreclosure, your country from decline. These and others—some very serious and well worth attending to, most far less so—all reinforce a fact so pervasive and obvious that it almost escapes consciousness: A lot of things in life need to be "fixed."

The Christian idea of salvation is about how to get life fixed at its most basic level. In this respect, Christianity is like every other religion. All religions take the position that however good life may be, still something fundamental is "out of joint" and needs to be repaired. Thus, they offer ways of correcting or transforming what has gone wrong. They provide a variety of paths to healing and health, "salves" of a fundamental and comprehensive nature that will remedy what is diseased. It may not be too much of a simplification to say that religion is about God (or Gods), God is about salvation, and salvation is about the most basic form of health.

The types of salvation offered within other religions parallel those offered within Christianity. Salvation, for example, is either spiritual or material in nature, for the individual soul or for individuals-in-community, for human beings or for all of creation, available in the present or in the future, forgiveness or transformation, a gift bestowed or a product of human seeking.

From the perspective of a progressive Christian vision no such choices can be made. Salvation includes all of the above.

Salvation through Christ

If a progressive Christian understanding of God is grounded in an interpretation of Jesus Christ, then so is an understanding of the salvation that God somehow makes possible. In other words, if our understanding of Jesus is the clue to our concept of God, it is also the clue to what salvation means. In chapter 3 we took the concept of incarnation as central to Christianity, as that concept is worked out in the christological councils and then applied to the audacious vision of salvation in Romans 8. The implications of this incarnational understanding of God for our view of salvation can be summarized in four points.

First, according to the Council of Nicea, the incarnate God, manifest in Jesus, is fully and truly God, not some lesser form of divinity. Thus, the salvation made possible by God incarnate is fully and truly salvation, not some preliminary or lesser form of healing. The real God makes possible real salvation.

Second, according to the Council of Constantinople, the full and true God is incarnate in the actual world, in ordinary humanity, and following Paul's vision in Romans, throughout the natural order. Thus, salvation is a possibility for the entire creation "as it is" including humans "as we are." The God incarnate in ordinary life makes salvation possible for ordinary people and the ordinary world.

Third, according to the Council of Ephesus, God is incarnate not only in, but also through, the creation. Thus, salvation is made possible not only in but also through the natural order of things. The God become incarnate in history through nature makes salvation possible through natural processes, both non-human and human.

Fourth, according to the Council of Chalcedon, in the incarnation full divinity and ordinary humanity are united "without division, without separation." Again, following the elaboration of the concept of incarnation implied by Paul, the process of divine salvation is one with the ordinary and natural processes of the world, without division, without separation.

If the term "natural" is understood expansively, and not in a reductionistic (i.e., mechanistic, deterministic, materialistic) manner, this progressive Christian view of salvation, like the view of God on which it depends, is a form of "Christian naturalism." But the better label for this progressive Christian perspective is a strictly theological one, "incarnationism." The God at home in this world saves this world through processes that are part and parcel of this world. Salvation is bringing the entire creation to fullness of health, not abandoning it. Salvation comes through the complex personal, political, social, and environmental processes of the created world, not in opposition to or distinction from them.

If traditional "otherworldly" views of salvation are difficult to comprehend, a "this-worldly" or incarnational view is scarcely less so. Developments in science continually remind us that we are far from understanding what "world" means. How then can we speak clearly about the salvation of the entire world? Explorations of personal, social, political, cosmic, and spiritual processes and their relationships are also embryonic. How then can we be clear about what would constitute their "health"? And when the inconclusiveness of these languages is added to the visionary character of theological reflection, it becomes apparent that talk of salvation will always be more than a little . . . well, imprecise! It will be imaginative talk, poetic talk. It will be metaphorical.

Two biblical metaphors, I believe, will be especially instructive for a progressive Christian understanding of salvation. One is the idea of the "kingdom" or (to use a better translation that eliminates the "kingly" overtones) the "reign of God." The other is the image of "eternal life." The former is central in the synoptic gospels—Matthew, Mark, and Luke—while the latter is central to the gospel of John. They are very different views, each intuiting distinctive aspects of the Christian hope for salvation. But they complement one another in interesting and important ways.

The Reign of God

There has been throughout Christian history a hope and belief that God's "reign" would come into the world as it is in heaven—or, in the language of the Lord's Prayer, that God's will would be done on earth. The metaphor of the reign of God implies that the world, which God created, is moving or will move toward some kind of fulfillment reflective of God's will. This expectation raises three questions: How will this "reign" come about? When will it come about? And what, concretely, would it mean for human life?

How this fulfillment will come about is portrayed variously in the biblical tradition. One group of views clusters around the "messianic" model. Although in later Christianity the concept of messiah took on supernatural connotations, earlier the messiah was an exceptional human leader who would rise up when the time was ripe and bring the divine reign into being. The coming of God's reign—the pervasive enactment of God's will for life in the world—would come about naturally, with human leadership, as the culmination of historical development. A second group of views builds on a very different model, one that is apocalyptic in character. The coming of God's reign would be a revolutionary intrusion into nature and history from the outside. It would be a radical break from all that had preceded it, instigated by a divine "son of man" who would "come down from above." Fulfillment would come through divine intervention into nature and history.

When will the reign of God occur? In the New Testament there is a consistent answer—that is, a consistently ambiguous answer. In the preaching of John the Baptist the kingdom is said to be "at hand." Similarly, Jesus, in the synoptic accounts, says the kingdom or reign of God "has come near to you" or "close to you" (Luke 10:9), or "is among you" (Luke 17:21). What these formulations clearly do not say is that the reign of God is internal and private, "within you," as Luke 17 has long been translated and is still commonly recited. But neither do they state a specific time—now, tomorrow, or in the more distant future. Instead they systematically blur the difference between present and future. New Testament scholars, therefore, typically characterize the reign of God as something that is always breaking in upon us but is never fully here. It is already, but always, in process. The reign of God, we might say, is the "always-future" that is already beginning to appear in our midst.

Finally, what is the reign of God? It is not a spiritual thing, or rather, not simply a spiritual thing. It is also social, political, and economic. It is human and non-human, individual and collective. In all of these dimensions of life, it is wholeness and fullness. The reign of God is, most succinctly, fullness of health throughout the whole web of life. Perhaps the most apt term for the reign of God in the Hebraic tradition is *shalom*, which means peace, but it is a peace that arises out of the interrelated health of things.

The biblical conception of the reign of God should form the core of a progressive Christian conception of salvation. Seeking salvation means seeking the healthful fullness of all the creation. Salvation comes into being (drawing on the messianic rather than the apocalyptic model) through this-worldly processes of nature, history, interpersonal relationships, and the dynamics of our individual lives. The reign of God, salvation, is always future, but equally it is always a future that is already breaking into our midst.

There is real salvation in this life. Furthermore, it is fully salvation, not some temporary or stopgap measure until a better "solution" for healing comes along. It is already breaking in upon us in the variety of ways that we celebrate and cherish—a request for forgiveness, a change of heart, a growth in love, a dedication to values beyond the self. It is coming among us in the father's nurturing love of his infant, the pastor's visionary leadership of her congregation, the educator's insightful exposure of racism, the corporate executive's insistence on fair employment practices, the labor leader's work on behalf of living wages, the citizen's defense of a sustainable environment. It comes near to us in legislative action that curbs bigotry, extends freedom, improves education, provides health care, encourages economic equality, recognizes the integrity of all the creation and promotes its well-being.

These—like Jesus' treatment of the Samaritan woman, his healing of the sick, his ministry among the outcasts, his overturning the tables of the money changers, and his assurance of forgiveness—are genuine "in-breakings" of salvation. In them and through them the incarnate God is working. Salvation, viewed from the perspective of the reign of God, is the process of bringing the creation, at any point and any time, toward the fulfilled and healthful community that is envisioned in the ideal of the two great commandments.

Eternal Life

The second biblical image of salvation, appearing in the Gospel of John, is the idea of eternal life. Contrary to what we might hear in church eternal life does not mean living forever. It is not about the "immortality" of the "soul." It is about a quality of the life lived in God. For the progressive Christian, it is the quality of a life lived in the incarnate reality of God.

The most important, and head-turning, part of the idea of eternal life is the insistence in John's gospel that eternal life is now: "Anyone who hears my word and believes him who sent me has eternal life, and does not come under judgment, but has passed from death to life . . ." (5:24). "Very truly, I tell you, whoever believes has eternal life" (6:47).

The life of one who believes in the God incarnate in creation has a distinctive character. It is not (necessarily) distinctive in virtue or knowledge; it is different because it is lived with a particular self-understanding. This difference is the character that a particular life takes on when it is lived as if it has been accepted ("assumed," to use the language of the councils) into the life of the incarnate God. Living in the world is also living in the God who has assumed the world. Eternal life is life suffused by that belief.

If the metaphor of the reign of God highlights the objective side of the Christian view of salvation, the image of eternal life emphasizes its subjective dimension. We sometimes speak of the latter as the experience of ultimate or abiding "meaning." Do our lives have some significance beyond what they contribute to the achievements of love in the web of creation? The answer implicit in the notion of eternal life is that they do. Our lives find a place in the life of the everlasting God who is incarnate in creation.

People and cultures come and go, mountains and seas appear and disappear, perhaps even worlds go in and out of existence. God is the creative good—person, principle, or process, all three ways of understanding God are employed by progressive Christians—that pervades the creation, seeking to move it toward more wholesome forms of order. What we do somehow makes a difference to God, contributes to the divine aims, adds to the divine life, enriches the divine experience. This is the "eternality" of our lives. Our lives have an everlasting meaning or worth as they find a place in the God who "assumes" them and all of life.

But there is a troubling downside to eternal life. Not only the good, but also the evil, as it happens, is accepted into God's reality. All that we do has permanence. Therefore, in a nonliteral but nonetheless disturbingly real sense, there is a hell as well as a heaven. Heaven is the permanence of every achievement on behalf of love, however partial, and the permanence of every action that contributes to that achievement, in the reality of God. But hell is real, too. It is the permanence of the good "that might have been, and was not."[11] Every destruction, every loss, every failure to love God, self, neighbor, and the rest of creation—these, too, are taken up as indelible facts in the being of an incarnate God.

Christians believe in divine grace, a grace that empowers and a grace that forgives. But forgiveness is not forgetfulness. Forgiveness is God's acceptance ("assumption") of our lives "in spite of" our failure to love, despite our destructive side. Divine grace makes sense only if there is some real meaning to "hell," and if grace is everlasting then so is failure. But, thankfully, we may also say the opposite: If failure is permanent, so is grace.

And what about "personal immortality"? Do we also contribute to God's life as we now contribute to each other, as dynamic and self-conscious selves? That is not precluded by the idea of eternal life. True, some theologians note that even in the New Testament it is God "alone [who] possesses immortality" (1 Timothy 6:16). Our desire for our own immortality, they say, is like the temptation of Eden; it is hubris, the longing to be like God. Even so, confidence in some sort of personal existence beyond death is part of the more common New Testament vision. Unlike the Greek idea of the immortality of the soul, however, in the biblical tradition existence beyond physical death is the continuation of the full person—not just the isolated, immaterial "soul"—in the environment of a new or renewed world.

Whatever we may think about personal immortality, the notion of "eternal life" is different. It is the claim that the ultimate meaning of our life is its contribution to, and its inclusion in, the reality of God. We diligently seek the coming reign of God in the world. The meaning of our labor is found not only there, but also, and abidingly, in the incarnate God whose purposes we serve. A life of fifty, five hundred, or an infinity of years gains its fundamental significance, not by its sheer longevity, but by its acceptance into the Abiding Life that everywhere and always seeks the good.

The Entire Created Order Set Free?

Christian talk of salvation would in any case be fragmentary, intuitive, metaphorical. It is especially so if that salvation is said, as Paul claimed, to encompass the "entire created order." This should not surprise us. All talk, of any sort, about a better world and the human role in bringing it about is the same—fragmentary, intuitive, metaphorical.

We speak of an end to racism without knowing exactly what that might mean in America or how, exactly, to bring it about. The goal is not precise, but it is clear enough to enable us to consider next steps and tentatively to anticipate those that might follow, and to pursue these steps together. We hope for a more humane economic order without knowing exactly how the respective strengths of capitalism and socialism might best be combined and their weaknesses overcome. The goal is not clear, but we know enough to begin to take steps that might bring about real—if still not fully adequate—change in American society. We do not "name the animals" by connecting dots on a page. We create more humane forms of order when the successes and failures of past ones are transformed into better visions—tentative, imperfect, vague, but better guiding visions.

Theological talk of salvation, too, is visionary; it, too, rests on metaphors, such as the "reign of God" and "eternal life." These and other characterizations of salvation are not literal descriptions. They are symbols; for us they seem to be givens, not sheer inventions, that reach into, and come from, the impenetrable depths of reality. In the cluster of these symbols we find intuitions of a better world that we mine like rich ore deep within the earth.

What we mine, however, is ore, not precise, finished products. We are never sure what the metals we mine can or will become. We take them out of the earth, examine them, imagine their possibilities, and work with them. We shape them into beautiful and valued guides to action for the time being. But these metals pre-existed our discovery of them by millions of years. They will live beyond the forms we give them, someday to become other, better guides—guides to the vision of an "entire created order" being set free from its bondage to sin, and more fully opened to the love of the incarnate God.

POINTS FOR REFLECTION

- Religions say that however good life may be, still something fundamental is "out of joint." It may not be too simplistic to say that religion is about God, God is about salvation, and salvation is about the most basic form of health.

- If Christology is the clue to our concept of God, it is also the clue to the salvation that God makes possible. The God

at home in the world saves the world through processes
that are part and parcel of this world.

- Two biblical metaphors are instructive for an understanding of salvation. One is the idea of the "reign of God." The
other is the image of "eternal life."

- The reign of God is fullness of health throughout the whole
web of life. It is already breaking in upon us through the
processes of nature, history, interpersonal relationships,
and through our individual lives.

- Eternal life is the quality of a life that is lived in the
belief that our world and our individual lives have been
"assumed" into the life of God. It is living in the incarnate
reality of God.

- In a nonliteral but disturbing sense, there is hell as well as
heaven. Heaven is the permanence of our every achievement on behalf of love in the everlasting life of God. Hell
is the permanence in God's experience of our every failure
to love.

- Christian talk of the "reign of God" and "eternal life" is
fragmentary, intuitive, metaphorical. These are guides to
the vision of an "entire created order" being set free from
sin and more open to the love of the incarnate God.

Chapter 8
Church:
Serving and Being Served

Progressive Christians join their liberal and conservative Christian friends in rejecting the agenda of the religious right as a poisonous departure from any credible interpretation of the gospel. Progressives will continue with liberals and authentic conservatives to name this poison for what it is—a repressive political ideology disguised in Christian trappings. However, without in the least diminishing the great value of liberalism and conservatism, progressive Christianity charts a different course. It is a course that takes the substantive importance of the biblical heritage much more seriously than has recent liberalism, and the substantive diversity of that heritage far more seriously than has conservatism.

This volume has presented one progressive Christian understanding of the Good News grounded in Jesus Christ. If it is acceptable, it provides a framework for articulating the Church's witness in the world, as well as a foundation for understanding the Church itself. The basic themes of this progressive perspective can be summarized in seven points.

A Progressive Christian Witness

1. *Progressive Christians* are people formed by the tradition grounded in Jesus Christ. Among the many religions that guide humanity, this tradition's heritage of myths, symbols, analyses, and convictions continuously nourishes our Christian understandings. The assertion of absolute truth for this tradition, or any interpretation of it, is contrary to Christianity's own best insights, as well as to the demonstrable fallibility of all human claims to truth. But we believe Christianity's historic resources offer vital criticisms, values, and visions that can provide insight, hope, and transformation today to the entire human family.

2. The *Bible* is our foundational resource. Its varied interpretations of Jesus Christ and the gospel "author" our identity as Christians. The diversity of these interpretations compels us to honor differences among Christians today. Their engagement with each other inspires us to engage our own differences, candidly but respectfully. The manifold voices within our scriptural foundation invite us into their dialog, criticize our limited understandings, teach us to think faithfully for ourselves, and empower us to come to views of our own about the meaning of Christian responsibility in today's world.

3. *Jesus Christ* discloses to us the oneness of God with the world and the manner of God's working in it. We share St. Paul's conviction that God seeks the salvation of the entire created order, and we share the conviction of the ancient Church that salvation is made possible by the power of

God's presence. Consequently we affirm the incarnation of God in the entire creation, not just humanity—fully God, fully at one with the full creation. Believing in Christ means believing that God is at home in the world, works through its processes, and is committed without reserve to its fulfillment.

4. The *God* revealed in Jesus Christ is the creative power for good at work in all of creation. God judges, heals, and transforms through persuasive love, not absolute power. Just as God makes a difference in the world, so we make a difference in the divine experience. God rejoices in our joys and suffers in our sorrows. We may experience the incarnate God as guide, presence, and mystery, but we can never capture God in our understanding. To claim absolute truth for any concept of God is a corruption of the religious standpoint, an expression of fear and a denial of faith.

5. *Humanity* is called to work with God in the service of the entire creation. Our responsibility is to use the resources given to us to create physical and social orders that enrich life at all its levels. Our guides are the Two Great Commandments—to love God and to love others as ourselves. The many other injunctions of Christian tradition, including Scripture's diverse and sometimes conflicting views, are instructive as the efforts of past generations to fulfill the commandments to love. That historic diversity, like diversity in the Church and world today, is a means by which the incarnate God guides our thinking and restrains our temptation to presume that we possess absolute truth.

6. *Sin* is thinking of ourselves—individually or collectively—more highly, or less highly, than we ought to think. Sin is the excessive valuing or disvaluing of any element, group, or portion of the creation in relationship to the rest. Our failure to love properly is sometimes the product of ignorance. More often we know what love requires but pretend otherwise. We deceive ourselves. Our failure to love properly and our self-deception about this failure create structures of inhumanity that continue from generation to generation. These structures—egotism, classism, racism, misogyny, homophobia, consumerism, nationalism, heterosexism, humanocentrism—abide as the environments in which we are formed from birth, and from which we must be set free.

7. *Salvation* is the activity of God incarnate, working through all of the processes of the creation to bring it to the fullness and health made possible by love. It is a promise for all dimensions of life—personal and social, physical and spiritual, human and non-human. Like all hopeful expectations, the comprehensive healing affirmed by Christian faith is visionary and thus metaphorical. The principle metaphors that frame the efforts of the progressive Christian are two-fold: the "reign of God"—a vision of this world transformed by justice and love, and "eternal life"—a vision of God incarnate in the world to whose reality our efforts and our lives might somehow contribute everlastingly.

8. The *Church* is . . . ?

Why the Church?

To explain how the Church fits into a progressive Christian vision it might be useful to begin with common experience, not theology. And it also might be beneficial (though troubling) if the examples from experience that we use show, by implication, the danger of the Church, as well as its importance. The examples I could give are numerous, but I will offer only two.

In the first, a former "interrogations" specialist serving with the military in Iraq recently reflected on why he was able to employ harsh techniques for questioning prisoners even though those methods were so clearly at odds with his upbringing and "normal" personal convictions. His explanation had to do with the communal experience of the interrogators themselves. They lived and worked together, he said, and that experience of community somehow created and sustained in them an acceptance of the "enhanced interrogation techniques" that most of them would previously have rejected, and which they again found to be abhorrent when they left their special communal reality.

The second example concerns a talk I had some years ago with a corporate executive about the extensive religious work he was doing with high school youth. I was particularly interested in the fact that so much emphasis was placed on intellectual formation, which in this case reflected a very conservative Christian perspective. He explained the course of study employed to create and sustain a particular point of view in the thinking and practice of these young people. I asked him whether the curriculum included exposure to alternative points of view. His answer was no. Naively, I asked why. He replied, "Because we want them to have a strong faith." A bit shocked, I pressed further, "But what happens when they go to college and encounter other viewpoints?" He replied that most of the young people will attend colleges that share that particular point of view, on scholarships from organizations that promote it, and for the rest of their lives attend churches in which that way of believing is the only lived reality.

These examples remind us that we "tend" (that's an understatement!) to become like those with whom we most consistently and closely associate, and we are sustained in those patterns by the continuing association. Or, to put the point more cryptically, we "are" those with whom we associate.

Beliefs and their related values are created and sustained most effectively in and through communal practices. The power of communities, according to theorists, resides in their complex meshing of mind and feeling, cognition and emotion. The intellectual dimension is essential, to be sure, but its capacity to direct and sustain a way of life depends on its integration with an affective dimension as well, particularly as manifest in the ritual life of a community. The rituals may be formal (the electoral process, or a religious liturgy) or informal (a neighborhood party, or coffee hour after worship). Rituals of either type enact—that is, express bodily—the ideas and beliefs central to a particular form of identity.

The power and sustainability of any worldview, religious or secular, depend first on there *being* a point of view—a standpoint comprised of specific ideas and beliefs that can be communicated and discussed. But that worldview depends no less (and perhaps even more so) on being rooted in a communal reality where ideas enter into and emerge out of—antiphonally, if you will—the emotional and actional life of the affections.

In some Christian liturgical traditions, for example, the Scripture lessons from the Old Testament and the New Testament epistles are read from the chancel of the church. Then, when it is time for the Gospel lesson to be read, the celebrants leave their elevated places, come down to the level of the worshippers, and read the Gospel there, among the people. For those who participate in this ritual enactment over time there can be no more powerful communication, at the level of feeling, of the meaning of the doctrine of the incarnation, the otherwise abstract idea that God has become one with us. When finally it is explained, the meaning of the incarnation of God is not so much learned as it is recovered, lifted out of the vast reservoir of feeling in which it has already found a home.

Like all other worldviews, whatever their focus, Christian concepts are clarified and sustained, as well as criticized and reconstructed, through varied forms of communal re-enactment. This communal grounding has a dangerous potential—a point to which we have already alluded and to which we shall return at the end of this chapter—but it is also essential for an effective Christian witness. Therefore, the social efficacy of a progressive Christian vision will depend to a very significant degree on its being grounded in the life of a vibrant communal reality where careful thinking, powerful ritual, and strategic action are intertwined.

This, from a sociological standpoint, is what the Church is for—to sustain an effective Christian vision. This is not theologically irrelevant from a progressive perspective centered on the incarnate God. God is at work, too, in social dynamics. But what else is the Church for, or more precisely, what else from a theological standpoint is the purpose of the Church? What should it be doing?

The answer to this question is usually derived from a view of the nature of the Church. What the Church should be, in most theologies, determines what the Church should do. If so, we must ask, what is the nature of the Church? The common answers are often elaborated as "models" or "images" of the Church.

Images of the Church

The earliest Christian communities and the earliest Christian understandings seem to have developed in tandem. Understandings produced communities, and communities produced Christian understandings. There were myriad examples of each, including numerous understandings of the Church. I recall in seminary hearing a professor claim that the New Testament contains as many as one hundred images of the Church. In most Protestant seminary textbooks today, however, the number has been pared down to three, four, or five.

One influential image is of the Church as the "people of God." This is a Christian adaptation of the idea of the Jews as God's chosen people. Progressive Christians will have problems with this image for a number of reasons. It is arrogant and more than a little triumphal—"Jews lost, Christians won, and now we are God's chosen people." We have seen the results of this kind of bias throughout Christian history.

There is a second reason to be suspicious of this image. Progressive Christians gratefully acknowledge God's presence in all of history, in all cultures, in all religions. So, from this perspective, all of us are "people of God," not just Christians. Finally, there is a factual problem with this model of the

Church. It suggests that of all people, Christians are the most "of God." What could that mean? Most godly? Most righteous? Unless we simply stipulate that "godly" or "righteous" means "being Christian," which is rather self-serving, it is difficult to substantiate a claim for our superior godliness. The Church is not the gathering of God's favored ones, from a progressive Christian perspective, nor does it appear to be those who are in fact the most like God.

In a curious way, however, there is a value in the notion of the Church as being special in some way. That value may be expressed in the way that some Jewish thinkers today have recast the notion of "election." Jews are elected, or "chosen," they say, not to a place of privilege, but to a particular task. The task to which Jews are chosen is to remind all of the world's people of the demands of justice. Election, in this understanding, is a special role, not a special status, and it does not preclude other groups also from having their own particular "vocation" in the world. This is an interesting idea, to which we shall return.

Another prominent image of the Church is as the "body of Christ." The organic motif in this image makes it quite attractive. The Church is intrinsically connected to the event of Jesus Christ. It does not simply remember that event, or celebrate it, or proclaim its significance, though it does these things, too. The Church somehow "embodies" this event. There are good and bad ways of thinking about embodiment. Positively, the Church is the bearer, in its own being, of an interpretation of the meaning of Jesus of Nazareth. That meaning is not a fact of history, it is not something discovered through historical investigation. The meaning of Christ is an interpretation of faith, and that faith interpretation resides in the Church. So the Church is the embodiment—in theology, ritual, and action—of the faith claim that, at the most fundamental level, "Jesus" means "God is truly, wholly, and radically incarnate in the world."

The negative construal of the Church as the "body of Christ" is obvious. Like the "people of God" motif, it is an invitation to think of the Church as somehow embodying a special virtue, in this case "Christ-likeness." It is possible to think this way only if one studiously ignores the messy facts of the actual Church! Even so, there might be something quite instructive about this view, if we were to keep in mind that "Christ" means the claim that God is incarnate in the world. The Church is the concrete location of that claim.

A third influential image is of the Church as the "community of the Spirit." Again, there are positive and negative sides to this image. On its behalf, we should note that it is tied to the understanding of salvation represented in the metaphor of the "reign of God" always coming into this world. The in-breaking of the reign of God was, in the biblical accounts, to be accompanied by the infilling of the Spirit of God. The idea of the Church as the "community of the Spirit" testifies to this hope for salvation "on earth as it is in heaven." But if it is taken to mean that the Church already possesses the Spirit, it is disastrous. It is disastrous because it is manifestly false, and in order to believe something so utterly false one must be more than mistaken, one must be delusional.

A fourth way of viewing the Church, also biblical in origin, is as the "servant people." At first glance there is not much to commend this view. No one likes to be a servant, and no one should. There was a different perspective on servanthood in the ancient world, but we don't need to accede to it any more than we accept its patriarchy, its hierarchy, or its affirmation of "humane" slavery. We are not called to be servants.

What about "service people," or "people who serve"? This is the most promising image for thinking about the Church, particularly if we recall the concept of "service" discussed in chapter 5. There we saw that the idea of human "dominion" or "lordship" is, in the example of Christ, transmuted into the role of "servanthood," but with the added connotation of cooperation rather than subservience. This balance, we noted, is nicely captured in the Jewish idea that humans are co-creators, or perhaps co-workers, with God in caring for the creation.

Service to the creation is not servitude. It is "naming the animals." This responsibility does not come with instructions to be followed mindlessly. It requires discernment, intelligence, imagination, and continual evaluation and revision. It is a vitally important responsibility. "Serving," I believe, yields an image of the Church that is most congruent with a progressive Christian perspective.

Seeking to Serve

The Church is the community of those who seek to serve God's healing work in the world, as that divine activity is understood in light of Jesus Christ.

Serving the Power that makes for healing is many-faceted. It requires a judgment about where the priorities are—who and what, in our time, are vulnerable. It requires an appraisal of how best to contribute to the healing needed in those particular contexts. It requires careful preparation to be able to contribute as needed. It requires implementing effectively the strategies that seem appropriate. But something still more basic is needed. Serving the Power that makes for healing requires sustained commitment—reflection, confession, repentance, affirmation, and resolution.

The Church's life is formed to call forth and sustain individuals-in-community who seek to serve the One who serves the world's healing. Through Scripture and tradition the Church recalls how this endeavor has been understood and undertaken in the past. Through its educational programs, the Church endeavors to learn from the past, identify the options, and to consider, discern, and clarify the forms of service needed today. Through preaching, the Church proclaims its mission, tests understandings of it, reflects on its dimensions, and calls Christians to commit themselves to seeking healing and being healers.

Organizing and planning in the Church is the process through which individuals and the community, usually under the guidance of a pastor, decide how to serve the Power that makes for healing. Evangelism is implementing the decision, sharing the good news that makes for healing. But what does "evangelism" mean to a progressive Christian? It means "extending the good news"—which is rather different than pronouncing condemnation on all who differ from you—in whatever form is appropriate to a particular situation.

Liturgy and worship are individual and collective processes of remembering, at the level of ritual action and inward feeling, the mission to which we are called, the reasons for our feeling called, and our commitment to this calling. It is re-enacting bodily—in song, silence, word, and gesture—all the elements of the Church's mission as that mission has evolved out of Scripture and tradition, education, preaching, organizing, and evangelism.

The Church, again, is the community of those who seek to serve God's healing work in the world, as that divine activity is understood through its ongoing interpretations of Jesus Christ.

"Seek" is the crucial word. Of course we will have successes, in ourselves, in our congregations, in our communities, in the world. But to claim too much for our successes is more than a little unwise. First, there is the problem of discerning how best to assist in healing. The complexity of brokenness even in our own hearts and relationships is staggering, and it becomes more so as we think about elements of "unhealth" in the social, economic, political, physical, and spiritual environments about us. Second, there is self-deception, the propensity to be dishonest, even with ourselves—no, especially with ourselves!—about what we do know and about what we can do.

There is another problem, a particularly pernicious form of self-deception. The very communal togetherness that is necessary in order to create, educate, and sustain Christian identity and commitment over the long haul—this absolute necessity . . . is also a grave danger. Congregations must forge agreements in order to act. But agreements all too easily become assumptions and assumptions become certitudes and certitudes become arrogance and arrogance becomes deafness to criticism and blindness to alternatives, leading to destruction.

In the Church's effort to serve salvation, its best hope for being saved from damning insularity is to remember that the God it aims to serve is in all the world. The world is where the incarnate Power is active. God is already there. Thus from each place to which we in the Church offer our transforming witness we should hope to receive a transforming witness we had not anticipated. From every group to whom we offer a prophetic critique we should be open to receive a critique that we need to hear. Every part of the world to which we bring healing might be for the Church a source of healing.

No, we should not claim too much. But neither should we hope for too little. We should not be so sure of the limits of the healing that is possible, even within ourselves. There is, after all, that persistent biblical witness to a Power at work among us that is able to do, in and through us, far more than we ask, more even that we can imagine is possible (Ephesians 3:20). For the world, for the Church, for us individually, the consequence of serving the God who makes "all things new" (Revelation 21:5) could be quite unexpected, and remarkable.

POINTS FOR REFLECTION

- Beliefs and values are sustained most effectively in communal practices that mesh thinking and feeling. The long term power of a progressive Christian worldview will depend on being integrated into the affective life of communities.

- The image of the Church as the "people of God" is arrogant and more than a little triumphalistic—"Jews lost, Christians won, and now we are God's chosen people."

- The image of the Church as the "body of Christ" rightly suggests that the Church somehow "embodies" the event of Jesus Christ. But it might also tempt us to believe that the Church embodies a special virtue, "Christ-likeness."

- The idea of the Church as the "community of the Spirit" testifies to the coming infilling of the Spirit of God. But if it is taken to mean that the Church already possesses that Spirit, it is disastrous.

- The Church as the "servant people" has unattractive connotations. Who wants to be a servant? But what about "service people" or "people who serve"?

- The Church is the community of those who seek to serve God's healing work in the world, as that divine activity is understood through its ongoing interpretations of Jesus Christ.

- We should not claim too much for the Church, but neither should we hope for too little. The consequences of serving the God who "makes all things new" could quite unexpected and remarkable.

Rightly Mixing Religion with Politics

Our nation desperately needs to hear reflective, value-laden voices on behalf of justice, repentance, inclusion, and healing. The richest repository of these voices is religion, and (though it has not been especially obvious during the past few decades!) in the United States the major repository of the voices we need to hear is Christianity.

Thus we are drawn to a rather uncomfortable question: "What?" as my brother emailed me recently, "Are you telling me we should have *more* religion in our national political debates?"

The answer is yes. We need more religion in our public discussions.

That is a counterintuitive and even dangerous claim, I know, because it can so easily be misconstrued or misused. So let me explain why I think religion-talk is appropriate and necessary in the public square of our pluralistic nation.

Mixing Religion and Politics

The historic view of political liberalism is that religious beliefs should be private matters, and that only "secular" (or supposedly neutral) values and reasons should be introduced into our public discussions. After all, we differ on religious issues, so it would seem sensible to assume that we must "bracket" our varied religious perspectives in order to find common ground on the contentious issues that confront us. "Let's keep our religions to ourselves"—that's the implicit rule of historic liberalism. In many ways, it has proven to be a fruitful maxim. Acceptance of it was a major factor in ending the religious wars of seventeenth-century Europe, and the violation of this maxim by right-wing Christianity in recent decades has introduced enormous division and strife into American public life.

There are good reasons, then, for urging that religion be kept out of politics. The only problem is that it is not possible, not if we think about the meaning of "politics" and "religion."

Politics is not simply political parties, candidates, and elections, though it includes those things. The term "political" comes from a Greek word "*polis*," referring to the ideal structure of community life. Our understanding of the political realm today reflects that original meaning; it has to do with the structure or organizational forms of our life together, the way our social life is constructed by both legislation and convention. Politics in the narrower sense is an important element of politics in the broader sense—those activities that pertain to the established or proposed patterns of communal relationships.

Religion is not simply creedal beliefs and ritual conduct, though it includes these. A religion functions as a fundamental orientation toward life. It is a framework for thinking about what is most important, and it is a way of living in accord with that thinking. Directly or indirectly, religion is the basis of a religious person's values and the beliefs related to those values. That is true of most expressions of Christianity and it certainly is true of progressive Christianity.

If "Keep religion out of politics" means "Don't bring your most basic values into public discussions about the organization of our life together," it is nothing less than telling the religious person to stay out of politics altogether! So separating religion and politics in this sense would disenfranchise people of faith, or it would encourage them to pretend something that is manifestly false—that their religious perspectives are unrelated to their judgments about public policies and public leadership.

Religious people cannot participate in our common public life without bringing their religion into this participation. That seems clear. But not all "mixing" of religion and politics is equal! There are good political reasons, and very good Christian reasons, for not bringing religion into our nation's political life in ways that lead to the warlike destruction of our communities—or, I should say, in ways that add to the destruction of our communities already begun in large part because of the mixing of religion and politics by the religious right. If we cannot avoid corrupting the democratic process with religion, as the Christian right has done, then we *should* be disenfranchised. But we can avoid undermining democracy—in fact, we can give voice to a Christian perspective that affirms and strengthens the democratic process. And we must!

The first step toward a wholesome mixing of politics and religion is to realize that religion is not necessarily the unique problem. It is not as if there is a religious sphere, on the one hand, that contains particular points of view that contradict what others might believe, and a secular sphere, on the other, that is neutral and ought to be acceptable to all. The secular perspective is not acceptable to everyone, nor, in fact, is it self-evidently true! So, from every particular perspective the question should arise: How can we properly advocate our particular point of view in a society where that viewpoint is not shared by all? The secular humanist, for example, should face this question as seriously as should the progressive Christian.

The second step is to realize that a secular perspective is not inherently anti-religious. Among current scholarly theories, a secular society is usually defined as one in which the various human enterprises (government, science, the economy, etc.) are differentiated or separated from each other, and all of them are freed from religious coercion. If that is secularism there are forms of almost every religion that are thoroughly secular! This includes major forms of modern Christianity, and clearly and unequivocally it includes progressive Christianity. The progressive Christian is as firmly committed as any other "secular" person to freedom from religious coercion, overt or subtle, in every sphere of life, including (we might note) the religious sphere.

The relationship of all of the differentiated and autonomous spheres, however, suggests something worth noting. They are separate and autonomous, but they are not unaffected by what goes on in other arenas. Government is separate from the economy, but neither is immune to the other's influence. Science is (or should be!) independent of government, but political decisions do influence science, as for example in the push to find technologies that will help curb global warming.

No sphere of life is hermetically sealed from the others. There is influence exercised properly, and, alas, influence exercised improperly. The same, I suggest, is true of the relationship of religion to other spheres of life, including its relation to politics. There is a role for the influence of religion in politics. It should not be to dictate political outcomes, either by fiat or by majority rule. But there is a role. What is it?

I will attempt to answer the question by offering six "rules" for bringing religion into our political discussions, focusing particularly on these rules as guides for the Christian.

Rules for Bringing Religion into Politics

1. Christians must accept the fact that our religious convictions are never, ever to be privileged over the convictions of others. Our views are never to be given advantage in the political process, never to enjoy preferential treatment because they are Christian. My grandmother used to say, "The ground is level at the foot of the cross." The ground is also level at the foot of the flag pole, or it should be.

There is a Christian reason for insisting on equity in our political debates. For Christianity in general it is our doctrine of creation, our view that God created the entire world in all of its tumultuous diversity, and pronounced it to be good. For progressive Christianity in particular it is also the belief that God is incarnate everywhere in the creation. Both beliefs mean that the imprint of the divine is present everywhere, and if we look carefully, it is to be found everywhere—in the multiple religions, in the diverse cultures, in the many ideological perspectives, and in the varied political perspectives.

No doubt the imprint of the divine is more muddled in some times and places than in others, but deciding that is a fallible human judgment to be made tentatively through a deliberative process, not at its beginning, and our decisions are always subject to critique and revision. The message of one Protestant denomination is "God is still speaking." Perhaps it should add, "And God's voice can come from anywhere." Christian convictions are never to be given preferential treatment in the political process, because Christianity itself warns us that we cannot assume we have a lock on the truth.

2. Christians must seek to understand our adversaries, and to be understood by them, but in that order. We need to try to place ourselves in the framework of others, whether our areas of agreement and disagreement are large or small. We must try to stand within their worldview. Their views may be strange, but in the biblical tradition strangers are to be welcomed for a very particular reason—because our relationship with them might bring about our mutual transformation.

We need to hear the stories of others—the secular humanists' stories of the Enlightenment and science, the Muslims' stories of the Prophet and the *hajj*, the Jews' stories of Torah and the land. We need to hear evangelicals tell how Jesus changed them and pentecostals tell how the Spirit filled them.

But, also, others need to hear our story. It is a startling story of God's oneness with the world, God's unreserved commitment to it, and a transforming story of the healing that this Oneness can bring to our brokenness. We must not be silent. We must say what in our heritage motivates us to be progressive Christians, to think as progressive Christians, to act as progressive Christians. Disagreements will remain, but in sharing our story, and hearing those of others, we can hope at last to become brothers and sisters who understand and respect one another, even when differences remain.

3. Christians should identify the many values that we share with others, and ask what we can build together on the basis of the things that we hold in common. This rule—that we should build on our commonalities—is an inheritance from secular liberalism, and it is worth keeping. We do not disagree on everything, and in fact our actual disagreements become exaggerated because we lose sight of what we share. What we hold in common should be kept at the forefront of consciousness even as we continue to debate other things.

From a progressive Christian perspective we will hold much in common because we are all creatures in whom God is incarnate. We may give different reasons for holding the same or similar values. Christians and atheists, Muslims and Jews, liberals and conservatives—they may have varying reasons for supporting democracy, ending racial injustice, defending freedom of the press, opposing the death penalty, advocating justice for homosexuals, protecting the environment, or whatever the cause. The difference in reasons or starting points, however, does not weaken the common resolve, especially if we share with one another the different journeys that bring us together. Our common values provide the basis for together seeking our common good.

4. Whenever possible, Christians must give as much ground as possible. In short, we must compromise. Compromise is the effort to allow room for our differences, to open space for as many alternatives as possible. It is a decision not to chisel

our particular conceptions of right and wrong into the hard rock of law.

There is a Christian reason for valuing compromise. It is the realization that we are all fallible, that none of us knows the pure will of God, that each of us is prone to hubris and self-deceit, and that the point of view of the other person, even if he or she is wrong, can perhaps provide a critique of our excesses, our short sightedness, our own insufficiencies. If politics is the art of compromise, compromise is the art of acknowledging that we are human. In Christian terms, compromise is a way of confessing that we are all creatures with partial perspectives; we do not know the absolute truth.

5. Christians should never press to outlaw conduct unless it directly undermines the common good. This abstract rule was implicit in the prayer I heard recently offered by a very conservative Christian. The prayer came at the end of a heated discussion on same-sex marriage, which he believes to be morally wrong but does not think should be outlawed. He prayed, "Dear Lord, we are thankful that we live in a country that allows people to do things we believe to be sinful." The underlying principle is this: Never seek to outlaw something because we think it to be immoral, or we find it to be offensive, unless it directly threatens the common good. In this case the common good was the institution of marriage. This conservative Christian said his marriage, and that of any truly mature couple, could not be weakened because of the marriage of gays and lesbians, even if he believed same-sex marriage to be sinful.

The law is for the purpose of extending rights, not restricting them, unless doing so is essential for the general welfare on which we all depend, as in the case of murder, malicious harm and exploitation, various forms of deceit, economic injustice, and so on. The Christian reason for defending the extension of rights, not their restriction, is the same as our allowance for compromise. Our ways are not God's ways, our thoughts are not God's, so a restriction on anyone's freedom requires special, careful justification based on what is broadly affirmed to be absolutely necessary for the maintenance of the common good.

6. Christians should deliberate in community. More precisely, we should deliberate in a community where enough unity exists to make conversation possible, and enough difference exists to make conversation valuable. Deliberate with others who understand even though they may disagree. We need to test our views, and that happens best with others who differ with us.

Christianity at its best is communal in character and diverse in the makeup of its communities. It is communal because only in community can its message be sustained over time. It is diverse because only in difference can its message be protected from the sinful presumption of infallibility. Do not deliberate alone; deliberate with others, in a community, where our convictions are shared openly and tested honestly in the fires of caring criticism.

When Rules are Not Enough, and Why

What if these rules don't work?

Of course they won't work, always. Many times they will fail, if failure means eliminating difference, always getting the errors of others replaced by what we believe to be right. And even if differences are resolved and agreements finally achieved, new disagreements will arise. Why?

An answer is suggested in Genesis 2. The human calling, we noted in chapter 5, is to "name the animals"—to continue the creation using human ingenuity, guided by the commandments to love. We have eyes for seeing the facts, hearts for feeling the needs, and minds for evaluating the alternatives. We do not have blueprints for deciding the precise ways that life should be ordered. In some cases there is no "right" way. In others, there are several imperfect but workable alternatives. In some instances there probably is a distinct "best" but we lack clarity about what it is. Searching together for the most appropriate way to order life, in light of all the relevant facts and moral concerns, is the slow and tumultuous process through which the incarnate God has chosen, in and through us, to continue the process of creation. This is how compassionate social structures are created and re-created. This is the human vocation.

It is not surprising, then, that our cultural processes, small and large, are tumultuous. Anthropologists used to think of a culture as a harmonious unity, much like a tree with single branches and limbs connected to a trunk and a single set of roots. Now they know better. A culture is not like a plant with parts that fit nicely together. A culture is an ongoing debate—like labor/management negotiations, or conservative/liberal political dialogues, or, as we well know, the painful struggles within our churches. Life together, in the church or outside of it, is a process of fallible creatures seeking ever more adequate ways of living with each other and with the earth. It is a turbulent process. That is what scholars who study cultural processes have come to understand. That is what Genesis 2 should have led us to expect.

Having differences is not a sign of failure, nor is our inability to resolve them readily or finally. The political struggles we have, in the church and in the broader culture, are part of the process of divine creation. In our differences we are, together, ordering and reordering the world.

Progressive Christians must be in the thick of this naming process, as one equal partner in the task, bringing our witness to current ecclesiastical and national deliberations, along with those of many others. We dare not be lulled into silence. Our Christian voice is vitally important. It endeavors to speak reflectively on behalf of justice, repentance, inclusion, and healing. The progressive Christian witness is "good news" for everyone.

POINTS FOR REFLECTION

- There are good reasons for urging that religion be kept out of politics. The only problem is that it is not possible. But not all "mixing" of religion and politics is equal.

- How can we properly advocate our point of view in a democratic society where that viewpoint is not shared by all? The secular humanist should face this question as seriously as should the Christian.

- My grandmother used to say, "The ground is level at the foot of the cross." The ground is also level at the foot of the flag pole, or it should be.

- We need to hear the secular humanists' stories of the Enlightenment and science, the Muslims' stories of the Prophet, the Jews' stories of the Torah, the evangelicals tell how Jesus changed them and pentecostals how the Spirit filled them.

- We do not disagree on everything, and our actual disagreements become exaggerated because we lose sight of what we share.

- If politics is the art of compromise, compromise is art of acknowledging that we are human. It is a way of confessing that we are all creatures with partial perspectives.

- Our ways are not God's ways, so a restriction on anyone's freedom requires special justification, based on what is broadly affirmed to be absolutely necessary for the common good.

- Having differences is not a sign of failure. The struggles we have in the Church and the broader culture are part of the process of divine creation. In our differences we are together ordering and reordering the world.

Notes

1. Gregory A. Boyd, *The Myth of a Christian Nation: How the Quest for Political Power Is Destroying the Church* (Grand Rapids, Mich.: Zondervan, 2006).

2. The authoritative history of liberal Christianity in America is now a trilogy by Gary Dorrien, *The Making of American Liberal Theology* (Louisville: Westminster John Knox Press, 2001, 2003, 2006).

3. Quoted in Donald W. Dayton, *Discovering an Evangelical Heritage* (New York: Harper & Row, 1976), 31–32, which is an excellent discussion of nineteenth-century evangelicalism.

4. For a brief, eminently readable discussion by an evangelical author, see Harry R. Boer, *Above the Battle: The Bible and Its Critics* (Grand Rapids, Mich.: Eerdmans, 1977).

5. Hannah Arendt, "What Was Authority?" in Carl J. Friedrich, *Authority* (Cambridge: Harvard University Press, 1958), 81–112.

6. James A. Sanders, *Torah and Canon* (Philadelphia: Fortress Press, 1972).

7. See Werner Foerster, "Exousia," in Gerhard Kittel, ed., *Theological Dictionary of the New Testament* (Grand Rapids, Mich.: Eerdmans, 1964), 562–74.

8. See "Rebellion," chapter 4, book 5, in Fyodor Dostoevsky, *The Brothers Karamazov* (New York: Bantam Books, 1970).

9. In addition to their own writings, a good introduction to Process and Openness theology is provided by a book that John Cobb and Clark Pinnock co-edited, *Searching for an Adequate God* (Grand Rapids, Mich.: Eerdmans, 2000).

10. Augustine, *Confessions*, 8. 5., in *Library of Christian Classics*, vol. 7 (Philadelphia: Westminster Press, 1955), 164–65.

11. Alfred North Whitehead, *Adventures of Ideas* (New York: Press Press, 1961), 286.